W9-ACX-832

ACTORS GUIDE TO MONOLOGUES
VOLUME 1 REVISED

JANE GRUMBACH
ROBERT EMERSON
EDITORS

DRAMA BOOK PUBLISHERS
NEW YORK

LIBRARY OF CONGRESS CATALOGING IN PUBLICATION DATA

Emerson, Robert.
    Actors guide to monologues.
    1. Monologues--Indexes. I. Grumbach, Jane,
joint author. II. Title.

PN4321.E5   1974   016.80882'45   74-23335
ISBN 0-910482-56-X (v. 1)
ISBN 0-89676-043-X (v. 2)

Printed in the United States of America

10 9 8 7 6 5 4 3 2   0   1 1 2 2   3 4 4 5 5 6 6 7 7 8 8 9 9

CONTENTS

INTRODUCTION

This book contains monologues from published plays only. Each entry lists the title and author of the play, the character's name and age, the approximate time of performance, the first line of the speech, and the act and scene in which it appears. For modern monologues, the character's exact age is given in brackets following the name. Nationalities are given where they apply in terms of accents.

A sample entry reads:

THE KNACK	Tolen	1:30	I	You mean how I get
Ann Jellicoe	(20, English)			women?* (SF 26)

The play is THE KNACK by Ann Jellicoe. The speaker is Tolen, aged 20, who has an English accent. The approximate performance time of the monologue is one minute and thirty seconds. The speech appears in Act I. The first line is "You mean how," etc. The asterisk (*) following the first line indicates that the monologue consists of two or more speeches pieced together. (SF 26) means that this monologue begins on page 26 of the Samuel French acting edition. The key to abbreviations of publishers' names is listed below.

For classical monologues, line numbers are given but not specific editions, as publications of these plays are so numerous. Please note that the line numbers given here come from the Washington Square Press editions. (The Greek tragedies are the Lattimore and Green translations; the Shakespearean plays are the Folger Library Editions.) However, line numbers should vary only slightly, so locating speeches in other editions and translations should present no problem.

For modern monologues, acting editions have been used wherever available, although most of these plays are also published in other editions. Dramatists Play Service, 440 Park Avenue South, New York City, and Samuel French, 25 West 45th Street, New York City, each sell their own editions only. The Drama Book Shop, 723 Seventh Avenue, New York City, and Theatrebooks, 1576 Broadway, New York City, sell all acting editions as well as all the other books listed in this guide. All of the plays--except for those published solely in acting editions--are available in paperback editions at bookstores all over the country.

KEY TO ABBREVIATIONS

ACC	–	Appleton–Century–Crofts
B–M	–	Bobbs–Merrill
Dram	–	Dramatic Publishing Company
DPS	–	Dramatists Play Service
HB	–	Harcourt Brace
H&W	–	Hill & Wang
NAL	–	New American Library
ND	–	New Directions
RH	–	Random House
SF	–	Samuel French
SFL	–	Samuel French Limited (England)
TDR	–	Tulane Drama Review

CLASSICAL FEMALE SERIOUS

YOUNG

PLAY Author	CHARACTER	TIME (approx.)	PLACE	FIRST LINE
AGAMEMNON Aeschylus	Cassandra	2:00	l. 1256	Oh, flame and...
ANTIGONE Sophocles	Antigone	2:00	l. 891	O tomb, O marriage...
ELECTRA Euripides	Electra	2:00	l. 112	Quicken the foot's rush...
ELECTRA Euripides	Electra	1:30	l. 299	I will tell if I must...
ELECTRA Sophocles	Electra	1:30	l. 87	O Holy Light...
ELECTRA Sophocles	Electra	2:30	l. 254	Women, I am ashamed...
ELECTRA Sophocles	Electra	1:30	l. 341	It is strange indeed...
ELECTRA Sophocles	Electra	2:00	l. 431	My dear one, not a morsel...
ELECTRA Sophocles	Electra	2:30	l. 558	I will tell you...
HENRY IV Part 1 Shakespeare	Lady Percy	1:00	II iii 38	O my good lord, why are...
IPHIGENIA IN AULIS Euripides	Iphigenia	3:00	l. 1211	O my father, if I had...
IPHIGENIA IN AULIS Euripides	Iphigenia	2:00	l. 1278	O pitiable am I...
IPHIGENIA IN AULIS Euripides	Iphigenia	3:00	l. 1367	Mother, now listen to my words.
THE LIBATION BEARERS Aeschylus	Electra	1:30	l. 183	The bitter wash has surged...
MEDEA Euripides	Medea	2:00	l. 214	Women of Corinth, I have come...
MEDEA Euripides	Medea	2:30	l. 365	Things have gone badly...
MEDEA Euripides	Medea	2:30	l. 465	O coward in every way...
MEDEA Euripides	Medea	2:30	l. 764	God, and God's daughter...
MEDEA Euripides	Medea	2:00	l. 869	Jason, I beg you to be...
MEDEA Euripides	Medea	3:00	l. 1021	O children, O my children...
THE MERCHANT OF VENICE - Shakespeare	Portia	1:00	III ii 42	Away then! I am locked...
THE MERCHANT OF VENICE - Shakespeare	Portia	1:00	IV i 189	The quality of mercy is not strained...
ORESTES Euripides	Electra	4:00	l. 1	There is no form of anguish...
ORESTES Euripides	Electra	2:30	l. 959	O country of Pelasgia...
PROMETHEUS BOUND Aeschylus	Io	2:00	l. 640	I know not how I should...

RICHARD III Shakespeare	Lady Anne	1:30	I ii 1	Set down, set down your honorable load...
ROMEO AND JULIET Shakespeare	Juliet	1:00	II ii 90	Thou knowest the mask...
ROMEO AND JULIET Shakespeare	Juliet	1:15	III ii 1	Gallop apace, you fiery-footed steeds...
ROMEO AND JULIET Shakespeare	Juliet	1:45	IV iii 15	Farewell! God knows when...
THE TROJAN WOMEN Euripides	Cassandra	1:30	l. 308	Lift up, heave up; carry the flame...
THE TROJAN WOMEN Euripides	Cassandra	3:00	l. 353	O mother, star my hair with flowers...
THE TROJAN WOMEN Euripides	Andromache	3:00	l. 634	O mother, our mother, hear me...
THE TROJAN WOMEN Euripides	Andromache	2:30	l. 740	O darling child I loved too well...
THE TROJAN WOMEN Euripides	Helen	2:30	l. 914	Perhaps it will make no difference...
THE WINTER'S TALE Shakespeare	Hermione	1:30	III ii 23	Since what I am to say must be but...
THE WINTER'S TALE Shakespeare	Paulina	1:15	III ii 193	What studied torments, tyrant...

MIDDLE-AGED

AGAMEMNON Aeschylus	Clytemnestra	3:00	l. 855	Grave gentlemen of Argolis...
ANTONY AND CLEOPATRA - Shakespeare	Cleopatra	1:00	IV xv 88	No more but e'en a woman...
ELECTRA Euripides	Clytemnestra	2:00	l. 1011	And dark and lonely were your father's...
ELECTRA Sophocles	Clytemnestra	1:30	l. 516	It seems you are loose...
ELECTRA Sophocles	Clytemnestra	1:00	l. 636	Phoebus Protector, hear me...
HENRY IV Part 2 Shakespeare	Lady Percy	1:45	II iii 10	O yet, for God's sake...
HENRY VIII Shakespeare	Queen Katharine	1:45	II iv 15	Sir, I desire you do me right...
IPHIGENIA IN AULIS Euripides	Clytemnestra	1:30	l. 899	Oh, you were born of a goddess...
IPHIGENIA IN AULIS Euripides	Clytemnestra	3:30	l. 1147	Hear me now...
MACBETH Shakespeare	Lady Macbeth	1:30	I v 1	"They met me in the day...

OLD

CORIOLANUS Shakespeare	Volumnia	2:30	V iii 147	Nay, go not from us thus.
RICHARD III Shakespeare	Queen Margaret	1:45	IV iv 92	I called thee then...
THE TROJAN WOMEN Euripides	Hecuba	2:00	l. 98	Rise, stricken head, from the dust...
THE TROJAN WOMEN Euripides	Hecuba	2:00	l. 466	No. Let me lie where I have fallen.
THE TROJAN WOMEN Euripides	Hecuba	3:00	l. 969	First, to defend the honor of the gods...

THE TROJAN WOMEN	Hecuba	2:00	I. 1156	Lay down the circled shield...
Euripides				

CLASSICAL FEMALE COMIC

YOUNG

AS YOU LIKE IT Shakespeare	Rosalind	1:15	III v 39	And why, I pray you?
AS YOU LIKE IT Shakespeare	Rosalind	1:45	V ii 28	O, I know where you are!
THE LEARNED WOMEN Moliere	Armande	1:00	I i 26	Lord, what a sordid mind your words...
LOVE'S LABOR'S LOST Shakespeare	Princess	1:00	V ii 889	A time, methinks, too short...
A MIDSUMMER NIGHT'S DREAM - Shakespeare	Helena	1:00	I i 232	How happy some o'er other...
A MIDSUMMER NIGHT'S DREAM - Shakespeare	Titiania	2:00	II i 65	Then I must be thy lady...*
THE MISANTHROPE Moliere	Celimene	2:00	III iv 913	Madame, do not misjudge my attitude...
MUCH ADO ABOUT NOTHING - Shakespeare	Hero	1:30	III i 51	O god of love!*
SCAPIN Moliere	Zerbinette	3:00	III iii	This has nothing to do with you...*
THE SCHOOL FOR WIVES Moliere	Agnes	2:00	II v	It's the most amazing story...*
THE TAMING OF THE SHREW - Shakespeare	Katherine	2:00	V ii 158	Fie, fie! Unknit that...
TWELFTH NIGHT Shakespeare	Viola	1:00	II ii 17	What means this lady?
THE WAY OF THE WORLD Congreve	Mrs. Millamant	1:45	IV i	My dear liberty, shall I leave...*

UNDER 20

PLAY Author	CHARACTER (Age)	TIME (approx.)	PLACE	FIRST LINE (Edition Page No.)
IN WHITE AMERICA Martin Duberman	Girl (15, Black)	2:45	II	The night before I was so excited...* (SF 62)
LOVERS (WINNERS) Brian Friel	Mag (17, Irish)	1:30	ep. 1	Everything's so still. (Dram 36)
THE STRAW - Eugene O'Neill - in "Six Short Plays"	Eileen (18)	1:45	II, 2	Then I want to say... (RH 96)

20 - 30

PLAY Author	CHARACTER (Age)	TIME (approx.)	PLACE	FIRST LINE (Edition Page No.)
ALL GOD'S CHILLUN GOT WINGS - Eugene O'Neill - in "Nine Plays"	Ella (20s)	1:45	II, 1	It's his Old Man... (RH 120)
ANDROCLES AND THE LION - Bernard Shaw	Lavinia (20s)	1:30	I	That is the strange thing, Captain... (Penguin 121)
ANNA CHRISTIE - Eugene O'Neill	Anna (20, Swedish)	1:00	III	I su'pose it I tried to tell you... (RH 134)
A BEAST STORY Adrienne Kennedy	Beast Girl (20s, Black)	1:00	1-act	My father comes to the door... (SF 36)
BIRDBATH - Leonard Melfi - in "Encounters"	Velma (26)	1:45	1-act	NOOOOOOO! YOU STAY AWAY...* (RH 34)
BLUES FOR MISTER CHARLIE James Baldwin	Juanita (20, Black)	2:30	III	He lay beside me on that bed... (Dell 124)
THE ENTERTAINER John Osborne	Jean (22, English)	1:30	sc. 3	Well, it's - oh, it's a complicated... (Dram 26)
EX-MISS COPPER QUEEN ON A SET OF PILLS Megan Terry	Copper Queen (26)	1:30	1-act	Hey there, Mister... (SF 51)
FLINT David Mercer	Dixie (20s, English)	2:30	II, 4	No sir, I have no means of support. (Methuen 72)
FUNNYHOUSE OF A NEGRO - Adrienne Kennedy	Negro (20)	2:30	1-act	Part of the time I live with Raymond... (SF 7)
GARDEN OF DELIGHTS Fernando Arrabal; tr: Bishop & Bishop	Lais (20s)	1:45	I	I don't want to... (Grove 40)
THE GINGHAM DOG Lanford Wilson	Gloria (27, Black)	3:00	II	I used to notice windows.* (DPS 52)
THE GINGHAM DOG Lanford Wilson	Gloria (27, Black)	1:45	I	I used to pray, I really... (DPS 41)
GOLD - Eugene O'Neill - in "Six Short Plays"	Sue (20)	1:30	II	It's something between Pa... (RH 147)
JUDITH Jean Giraudoux	Judith (20s, Israeli)	1:30	II	Is it you, is it Daria? (DPS 43)
LAZARUS LAUGHED Eugene O'Neill - in "Nine Plays"	Pompeia (20s)	1:45	IV, 1	No! No! It is... (RH 470)
LOOK BACK IN ANGER John Osborne	Alison (25, English)	1:00	III, 2	It doesn't matter. I was wrong. (Dram 78)
LOOK HOMEWARD, ANGEL Ketti Frings	Laura (23)	1:30	III	Mrs. Gant, this isn't easy. (SF 80)
MIDDLE OF THE NIGHT Paddy Chayefsky	The Girl (24)	2:00	I, 3	It just burst out of me.* (SF 21)

MISS JULIE August Strindberg	Julie (25)	1:30	1-act	No, I won't go yet. (Avon 65)
RING ROUND THE MOON Jean Anouilh	Isabelle (20s)	1:00	III, 1	Well, are you satisfied now? (DPS 63)
THE SEA GULL Anton Chekhov	Nina (20s)	2:30	IV	Why do you say you kiss the ground...* (SF 59)
SHELTER Alun Owen	Girl (late 20s)	2:00	2	Mean, petty, cheap, calculating. (SFL 19)
SLAG David Hare	Joanne (23, English)	1:15	2	Let me make... (Faber 34)
STRANGE INTERLUDE Eugene O'Neill - in "Three Plays"	Nina (21)	2:30	Pt 1, Act III	It's a queer house, Ned. (RH 98)
STRANGE INTERLUDE Eugene O'Neill - in "Three Plays"	Nina (23)	2:30	Pt 1, Act V	There! That can't be my imagination... (RH 132)
STREET SCENE Elmer Rice	Rose (20)	1:45	III	I like you so much, Sam.* (SF 233)
TAKE A GIANT STEP Louis Peterson	Christine (late 20s, Black)	1:30	II, 2	My father was killed in the mills...* (SF 72)
A TOUCH OF THE POET Eugene O'Neill	Sara (20, Irish-Am.)	4:30	IV	Oh, mother, it's a great joke on me.* (Yale 144)
U.S.A. - John Dos Passos & Paul Shyre	Player F (any age)	5:00	II	In San Francisco in 1878, Mrs. Isadora... (SF 63)
WE RIGHTEOUS BOMBERS Kingsley Bass - in "Black Drama in America: an Anthology"	Sissie (20s, Black)	1:15	II	I'm sorry...I'm sorry, brothers... (Fawcett 578)

30-40

APPROACHING SIMONE Megan Terry	Simone (30)	2:45	II	We're in a conflict... (Feminist 125)
BETWEEN TWO THIEVES Warner LeRoy	Blonde (30)	1:30	II	No. I'm not an actress. (SF 56)
CAT ON A HOT TIN ROOF Tennessee Williams	Margaret (30, Southern)	2:00	I	I know, believe me, I know that... (DPS 27)
DESIRE UNDER THE ELMS Eugene O'Neill - in "Three Plays"	Abbie (35)	1:30	I, 4	If cussin' me does... (RH 21)
FATHER'S DAY Oliver Hailey	Estelle (30s)	1:15	II	I admire Marian very much. (DPS 58)
HELLO AND GOODBYE Athol Fugard	Hester (30s, White South African)	1:45	I	Not like that. Maybe frightened... (SF 13)
HELLO AND GOODBYE Athol Fugard	Hester (30s, White South African)	1:00	II	They pushed me forward. (SF 46)
THE JEWISH WIFE Bertold Brecht	The Wife (36, Jewish)	3:30	1-act	Yes, I'm going now, Fritz. (Grove 13)
JOE EGG Peter Nichols	Sheila (35, English)	3:00	I	I join in these jokes to please him. (Grove 44)
JOE EGG Peter Nichols	Sheila (35, English)	1:30	I	One of these days I'll hit him. (Grove 26)
NO EXIT Jean-Paul Sartre	Estelle (30s)	2:00	1-act	Hah! Mine? All right, which one... (SF 37)
OLD JUDGE MOSE IS DEAD Joseph White	Miss Jane (34, Black)	1:30	1-act	Oh, daddy, daddy, I'll miss... (TDR 40 - p. 155)
ORPHEUS DESCENDING Tennessee Williams	Carol (30s, Southern)	1:30	I, 2	I used to be what they call a... (DPS 19)

Play / Author	Character	Time	Act/Scene	First Line
THE OWL ANSWERS Adrienne Kennedy - in "Cities in Bezique"	She (34, Black)	1:30	1-act	Communications, God, communications... (SF 22)
THE OWL ANSWERS Adrienne Kennedy - in "Cities in Bezique"	She (34, Black)	1:45	1-act	He came to me in the outhouse... (SF 15)
THE PETRIFIED FOREST Robert Sherwood	Mrs. Chisholm (35)	1:15	II	You haven't the remotest... (DPS 60)
SNOWANGEL - Lewis John Carlino - in "Cages"	Connie (30s)	1:30	1-act	He came to me while I was... (DPS 24)
STRANGE INTERLUDE Eugene O'Neill - in "Three Plays"	Nina (35)	1:00	Pt 2, Act 7	No longer my baby... (RH 171)
A STREETCAR NAMED DESIRE - Tennessee Williams	Blanche (30s, Southern)	1:30	I, 1	I, I, I took the blows... (DPS 16)
A STREETCAR NAMED DESIRE - Tennessee Williams	Blanche (30s, Southern)	1:45	II, 2	He was a boy, just a boy... (DPS 67)
TALK TO ME LIKE THE RAIN AND LET ME LISTEN Tennessee Williams - in "27 Wagons Full of Cotton"	Woman (30s)	4:30	1-act	I will receive a check... (ND 216)
TO BE YOUNG, GIFTED AND BLACK - Robert Nemiroff	First actress (30s, Black)	1:15	I, 7	Harlem church, a Baptist church. (SF 54)
TO BE YOUNG, GIFTED AND BLACK - Robert Nemiroff	First actress (30s, Black)	1:45	II, 1	April 27, 1962. Dear Kenneth... (SF 71)
THE WHITE WHORE AND THE BIT PLAYER - Tom Eyen - in "New American Plays, vol. 2"	The Nun (30s)	1:25	1-act	Put away, dear! (H&W 232)
WINE IN THE WILDERNESS Alice Childress	Tommy (30s, Black)	1:30	1-act	I don't stay mad...* (DPS 37)

40 - 60

Play / Author	Character	Time	Act/Scene	First Line
THE ADDING MACHINE Elmer Rice	Mrs. Zero (45)	5:30	sc. 1	I'm gettin' sick o' them Westerns. (SF 1)
CAMINO REAL Tennessee Williams	Marguerite (40s)	1:30	Block 10	Oh, Jacques, we're used to each other... (DPS 63)
CHAMBER MUSIC - Arthur Kopit - in "The Day the Whores Came Out to Play Tennis..."	Woman in Aviatrix's Outfit (40s)	1:00	1-act	All right, check the records... (H&W 12)
THE CHERRY ORCHARD Anton Chekhov	Lyuboff (40s)	2:00	III	What truth? You see where the... (SF 59)
DEAR LIAR Jerome Kilty	Mrs. Campbell (40s, English)	1:15	II	There! It is just this... (SF 39)
DEAR LOVE Jerome Kilty	Elizabeth (40, English)	2:30	I	Mr. Browning, I am accustomed... (SF 21)
EQUUS Peter Shaffer	Dora (40s, English)	2:30	sc. 23	Look, Doctor... (Deutsch 75)
EXIT THE KING Eugene Ionesco	Marguerite (40)	2:30	1-act	He can still distinguish colors. (Grove 93)
FIVE FINGER EXERCISE Peter Shaffer	Louise (40s, English)	2:30	I, 2	I'm not a very happy person...* (SFL 27)
THE GINGERBREAD LADY Neil Simon	Toby (early 40s)	1:00	III	You're not twenty-two... (SF 68)

Title / Author	Character	Time	Act/Scene	Opening Line
THE GLASS MENAGERIE Tennessee Williams	Amanda (50s, Southern)	1:30	II, 7	It used to be. It used to be. (DPS 43)
HALLOWEEN - Leonard Melfi - in "Encounters"	Margaret (50)	1:00	1-act	Don't be smart, young man. (RH 92)
INADMISSIBLE EVIDENCE John Osborne	Mrs. Garnsey (40s, English)	1:30	I	I don't know.* (Dram 74)
LONG DAY'S JOURNEY INTO NIGHT - Eugene O'Neill	Mary (54, Irish-American)	2:30	III	It kills the pain. (Yale 104)
LONG DAY'S JOURNEY INTO NIGHT - Eugene O'Neill	Mary (54, Irish-American)	2:30	III	No, dear. But I forgive.* (Yale, 114)
LONG DAY'S JOURNEY INTO NIGHT - Eugene O'Neill	Mary (54, Irish-American)	1:15	IV	I had a talk with Mother Elizabeth. (Yale 175)
LOOK AWAY Jerome Kilty	Mary (56)	3:00	I	Doctors, you say... (SF 7)
LOOK AWAY Jerome Kilty	Elizabeth (middle-aged, Black)	3:30	I	Elizabeth Keckley...* (SF 9)
LOOK HOMEWARD, ANGEL - Ketti Frings	Eliza (57)	1:45	III	Well, I'll deposit the money...* (SF 89)
MOURNING BECOMES ELECTRA - Eugene O'Neill - in "Three Plays"	Christine (40)	1:30	"The Hunted" I, 1	Vinnie, I - I must... (RH 289)
MOURNING BECOMES ELECTRA - Eugene O'Neill - in "Three Plays"	Christine (40)	2:00	"The Hunted" II	Well, you can go... (RH 301)
THE MUTILATED Tennessee Williams	Trinket (50)	2:00	sc. 2	Such a clear, frosty night... (DPS 20)
A PALM TREE IN A ROSE GARDEN - Meade Roberts	Rose (50s)	3:30	II, 1	On a summer afternoon, I won... (DPS 38)
PORTRAIT OF A MADONNA Tennessee Williams - in "27 Wagons Full of Cotton"	Miss Collins (middle-aged, Southern)	2:30	I	I left my parasol once... (ND 99)
THE ROSE TATTOO Tennessee Williams	Serafina (early 40s, Italian)	1:00	I, 5	I count up the nights... (DPS 33)
SATURDAY, SUNDAY, MONDAY - Eduardo de Filippo - adapt: Waterhouse & Hall	Rosa (50s)	2:15	II	Giuliane, come here. (Heinemann 59)
THE SLAVE LeRoi Jones	Grace (40)	1:30	1-act	What? Is no one to... (Morrow 67)
THE SUBJECT WAS ROSES Frank D. Gilroy	Nettie (45)	2:00	II, 3	I think it was his energy... (SF 64)
SUMMERTREE Ron Cowen	Mother (40s)	1:30	II	You know, when it comes... (DPS 29)
SWEET BIRD OF YOUTH Tennessee Williams	Princess (middle-aged)	1:15	I, 1	For years they all told me that... (DPS 18)
SWEET BIRD OF YOUTH Tennessee Williams	Princess (middle-aged)	1:30	III	Why did I give him the number? (DPS 55)
A TOUCH OF THE POET Eugene O'Neill	Deborah (41)	2:00	II	It is natural you should admire that... (Yale 82)
A TOUCH OF THE POET Eugene O'Neill	Nora (40, Irish)	2:30	IV	Ah, it's you, darlin'! (Yale 136)
WELCOME TO ANDROMEDA - Ron Whyte	Nurse (40s)	1:45	1-act	He took two knitting... (SF 37)
WHO'S AFRAID OF VIRGINIA WOOLF? Edward Albee	Martha (45)	2:15	III	Hey, hey... Where is... (DPS 86)

ANASTASIA Marcelle Maurette	Empress (70s, Russian)	1:00	II	Malenkaia! Malenkaia! (SF 64)
THE BOY IN THE BASEMENT William Inge - in "Eleven Short Plays"	Mrs. Scranton (70s)	1:15	1-act	You got them when you went there... (DPS 48)
THE ENTERTAINER John Osborne	Phoebe (60, English)	2:15	sc. 6	You don't know what it's like.* (Dram 49)
JOE EGG Peter Nichols	Grace (65, English)	2:00	II	No, well I wouldn't have... (Grove 65)
LAZARUS LAUGHED Eugene O'Neill - in "Nine Plays"	Miriam (old)	1:30	III, 2	Say what you like... (RH 454)
THE LOVES OF CASS McGUIRE - Brian Friel	Cass (70, Irish)	1:15	II	Hi, I made damn sure... (SF 30)
THE MAN IN THE GLASS BOOTH - Robert Shaw	Old Woman (German)	2:30	II	I have sat and sat. (SF 55)
THE ROOM Harold Pinter	Rose (60, English)	3:45	1-act	Here you are. This'll keep the cold out. (SFL 1)
THE WARNING-A THEME FOR LINDA - Ronald Milner - in "A Black Quartet"	Grandmother (old, Black)	1:30	sc. 3	Well, sir, I was scared to look... (NAL 104)
WATERCOLOR Philip Magdalany	Diane (old)	1:30	1-act	You're lying. I know it. (DPS 47)

MODERN FEMALE COMIC

UNDER 20

AFTER HAGGERTY David Mercer	Claire (17, English)	2:15	II, 3	James Mawnan Haggerty, I'm going... (Methuen 61)
THE EFFECT OF GAMMA RAYS ON MAN-IN-THE- MOON MARIGOLDS Paul Zindel	Janice (16)	1:15	II, 2	The Past. I got the cat... (DPS 39)
FEIFFER'S PEOPLE Jules Feiffer	Little Girl	1:15	-	So I was standing on the corner... (DPS 77)
HAPPY BIRTHDAY, WANDA JUNE - Kurt Vonnegut, Jr.	Wanda June (8)	1:15	I, 4	Hello. I am Wanda June. (Dell 53)
LOVERS (WINNERS) Brian Friel	Mag (17, Irish)	1:45	episode 1	I can see the boarders... (Dram 23)
RALLY ROUND THE FLAG, BOYS! - David Rogers	Comfort (16)	1:15	I, 1	Dear Elvis, I suppose you're... (Dram 18)
SLOW DANCE ON THE KILLING GROUND William Hanley	Rosie (18)	2:15	II, 1	If you knew me better... (DPS 41)

20 - 30

AFTER HAGGERTY David Mercer	Claire (late 20s)	2:30	II, 5	Don't say it, Haggerty! (Methuen 72)
THE BALD SOPRANO Eugene Ionesco - in "Four Plays"	Mary (20s)	1:15	1-act	Elizabeth and Donald are now... (Grove 19)

BLUES FOR MISTER CHARLIE James Baldwin	Jo (20s)	1:15	III	Am I going to spend the rest... (Dell 110)
FEIFFER'S PEOPLE Jules Feiffer	Young girl (20)	1:00	-	Try to see it my way. (DPS 41)
INFANCY Thornton Wilder	Millie (20s)	1:00	1-act	Moe! What's the matter... (SF 16)
IN WHITE AMERICA Martin Duberman	Eliza (20s, Southern)	1:30	II	Washington, Georgia. No power... (SF 39)
JUMPERS Tom Stoppard	Dotty (late 20s, English)	1:30	I	And yet, Professor...* (Grove 35)
JUMPERS Tom Stoppard	Dotty (late 20s, English)	1:15	II	Well, it's all over... (Grove 74)
LITTLE MURDERS Jules Feiffer	Patsy (27)	2:30	II, 1	Screaming! You son of a bitch...* (SF 42)
LUNCHTIME - Leonard Melfi - in "Encounters"	Avis (25)	1:30	1-act	When I first met George... (RH 66)
LUNCHTIME - Leonard Melfi - in "Encounters"	Avis (25)	1:30	1-act	Would you like ham? (RH 70)
NEXT TIME I'LL SING TO YOU - James Saunders	Lizzie (20s)	3:00	II	I suppose so. Not that I'm... (DPS 40)
NOON - Terrence McNally - in "Morning, Noon, and Night"	Allegra (early 20s)	2:45	1-act	Bonjour! Bonjour! (SF 65)
OH, MEN! OH, WOMEN! Edward Chodorov	Mildred (20s)	7:30	I	Well - I awakened Miss Tacher...* (SF 31)
THE PUBLIC EYE Peter Shaffer	Belinda (22, English)	2:30	1-act	All right....First let me tell you...* (SF 32)
ROMANOFF AND JULIET Peter Ustinov	Juliet (20s)	1:30	II	Oh, why must the mind... (DPS 35)
THE SKIN OF OUR TEETH Thornton Wilder	Sabina (early 20s)	3:00	I	Oh, oh, oh! Six o'clock... (SF 10)
THE STAR-SPANGLED GIRL Neil Simon	Sophie (23, Southern)	1:30	I, 2	Mr. Cornell, oh have tried... (DPS 20)
THE STAR-SPANGLED GIRL Neil Simon	Sophie (23, Southern)	1:15	I, 2	Two years ago in Japan... (DPS 23)
THOUGHTS ON THE INSTANT OF GREETING A FRIEND ON THE STREET - Jean-Claude van Itallie & Sharon Thie - in "Collision Course"	Woman (20s)	1:30	1-act	I really loved this guy... (RH 81)
TIMES SQUARE - Leonard Melfi - in "Encounters"	Bobo (20s)	1:30	1-act	Lovers on Forty-second Street. (RH 184)
TIMES SQUARE - Leonard Melfi - in "Encounters"	Marigold (early 20s)	2:45	1-act	My name is Marigold...* (RH 191)
TIMES SQUARE - Leonard Melfi - in "Encounters"	Laura Jean (early 20s, Southern)	1:30	1-act	I want you to kiss me... (RH 197)
THE TYPISTS Murray Schisgal	Sylvia (20s)	1:15	1-act	My family never had money problems. (DPS 12)

30 - 40

CHAMBER MUSIC - Arthur Kopit - in "The Day the Whores Came Out to Play Tennis..."	Woman in Safari Outfit (30s)	1:00	1-act	You see, I've spent...* (H&W 25)
CUBA SI! Terrence McNally	Cuba (30s, Cuban)	1:30	1-act	Bastard. Dirty hooligan bastard. (DPS 7)
FATHER'S DAY Oliver Hailey	Louise (30s)	1:00	I	Well, suppose I get it... (DPS 14)

FEIFFER'S PEOPLE Jules Feiffer	Miss Sacrosanct (30s)	1:30	-	Hello, is this Mr. Mergendeiler? (DPS 57)
HAPPY ENDING Douglas Turner Ward	Ellie (late 30s, Black)	1:15	1-act	I cook the food, scrub the floor... (DPS 17)
THE HOUSE OF BLUE LEAVES - John Guare	Bunny (39)	1:30	I	I'm not that kind of girl.* (SF 15)
NOT ENOUGH ROPE Elaine May	Edith (25-35)	1:45	1-act	Look, I lied about the rope. (SF .13)
OBJECTIVE CASE Lewis John Carlino	She (30)	1:30	1-act	Allow me to introduce myself. (DPS 40)
THE PRIME OF MISS JEAN BRODIE - Jay Allen	Brodie (35, English)	2:00	I, 2	Little girls. I am in the business... (SF 7)
SCUBA DUBA Bruce Jay Friedman	Jean (early 30s)	1:45	II	Harold, will you just listen...* (DPS 40)

40 AND OVER

COME BLOW YOUR HORN Neil Simon	Mother (50s, Jewish)	2:15	II	Hello? Who? (SF 44)
THE GNADIGES FRAULEIN Tennessee Williams	Polly (40s, Southern)	3:00	1-act	Was that two cocaloony birds... (DPS 5)
THE GNADIGES FRAULEIN Tennessee Williams	Molly (40, Southern)	2:30	1-act	WHY! - He regarded her... (DPS 30)
INVITATION TO A MARCH Arthur Laurents	Camilla (40s)	1:45	III	Sit down and shut up! (DPS 65)
LAST OF THE RED HOT LOVERS - Neil Simon	Jeanette (40)	1:30	III	Do you know Charlotte Korman...* (SF 66)
LOVERS AND OTHER STRANGERS - Renee Taylor & Joseph Bologna	Bea (45-55)	1:15	4	And Joan, of all the pictures... (SF 40)
LOVERS AND OTHER STRANGERS - Renee Taylor & Joseph Bologna	Bea (45-55)	1:30	4	Well, here it is...* (SF 42)
OH DAD, POOR DAD, MAMMA'S HUNG YOU IN THE CLOSET AND I'M FEELIN' SO SAD - Arthur Kopit	Madame Rosepettle (40s)	10:00	sc. III	Now you don't really want to leave...* (SF 39)
PHOTO FINISH Peter Ustinov	Stella (old)	2:15	I	Now...no...yes... (DPS 5)
PLAZA SUITE Neil Simon	Norma (middle-aged)	1:30	III	Hello?...Hello, operator? (SF 71)
SCENES FROM AMERICAN LIFE - A.R. Gurney, Jr.	Woman (40s)	1:15	I	Um. I want to make... (SF 32)
A SLIGHT ACHE - Harold Pinter - in "Three Plays"	Flora (middle- aged, English)	4:00	1-act	I shall wave from the window... (Grove 30)

MODERN FEMALE SERIO-COMIC

20 - 30

BIRDBATH - Leonard Melfi - in "Encounters"	Velma (26)	1:30	1-act	Well, sometimes Mr. Quincy... (RH 9)
THE DAYS AND NIGHTS OF BEEBEE FENSTERMAKER William Snyder	Beebee (20s, Southern)	4:00	III	"When where you are is where... (DPS 60)

FIVE ON THE BLACK HAND SIDE - Charlie L. Russell	Gail (20, Black)	1:15	I, 1	Daddy is such a phony.* (SF 11)
FLINT David Mercer	Dixie (20s, English)	1:00	II, 1	The Liverpool Irish are clingers. (Methuen 52)
A MOON FOR THE MISBEGOTTEN - Eugene O'Neill	Josie (28, Irish)	1:45	III	That's right. Do what... (RH 99)
THE TIME OF YOUR LIFE William Saroyan	Kitty (20s)	1:00	I	I dream of home. (SF 34)
THE WARM PENINSULA Joe Masteroff	Ruth (20s)	2:00	I	They say all brides are... (SF 5)
THE WARM PENINSULA Joe Masteroff	Joanne (20s)	1:00	I	There are a couple of cities... (SF 6)

30 - 40

FATHER'S DAY Oliver Hailey	Marian (30s)	1:00	I	That's wonderful, Estelle. (DPS 20)
THE GOOD DOCTOR Neil Simon	Wife (30s)	2:00	I, 6	No! Not a word! (RH 61)
JOE EGG Peter Nichols	Pam (30s, English)	2:00	II	It wasn't my idea... (Grove 62)
OLD TIMES Harold Pinter	Kate (30s, English)	2:30	II	But I remember you. (Grove 71)
THE PRIME OF MISS JEAN BRODIE - Jay Allen	Brodie (35, English)	2:15	II, 5	I will not resign... (SF 57)
WHAT SHALL WE TELL CAROLINE? - John Mortimer	Lily (30s, English)	2:45	1-act	Caroline, they try to tell you... (SFL 31)

40 - 60

A BREEZE FROM THE GULF Mart Crowley	Loraine (40s)	2:00	I, 3	Daddy and I had...* (SF 21)
DEAR LIAR Jerome Kilty	Mrs. Campbell (40s, English)	1:30	II	New York, August 1937... (SF 51)
THE EFFECT OF GAMMA RAYS ON MAN-IN-THE-MOON MARIGOLDS Paul Zindel	Beatrice (45)	3:00	I, 2	Science, science, science! (DPS 18)
THE FOURPOSTER Jan de Hartog	She (40s)	1:30	III, 1	I didn't intend to say... (SF 49)
THE GINGERBREAD LADY Neil Simon	Evy (40s)	1:30	I	You're seventeen years old...* (SF 28)
JOHNNAS Bill Gunn	Hilly (middle-aged, Black)	3:00	—	I love him...I don't know how he... (TDR 40 p. 130)
MALCOLM Edward Albee	Madame Girard (middle-aged)	1:30	II, 4-5	I understand - though one is never sure... (DPS 52)
THE MATCHMAKER Thornton Wilder	Mrs. Levi (uncertain age)	2:30	IV	Ephraim Levi, I'm going to get married... (SF 109)

60 AND OVER

FLINT David Mercer	Victoria (mid-60s, English)	2:30	II, 2	I had such a lovely dream. (Methuen 62)
THE LION AND THE JEWEL Wole Soyinka	Sadiko (old, Black)	1:15	Night	So we did for you too did we? (Oxford 32)
ONCE UPON A SEASHORE Donald East	Josephine (old)	1:45	1-act	Oh, I was a bitch. (SFL 10)

CLASSICAL MALE SERIOUS

YOUNG

PLAY Author	CHARACTER	TIME (approx.)	PLACE	FIRST LINE
ANTIGONE Sophocles	Haemon	2:00	l. 685	Father, the gods have given men good sense...
ELECTRA Euripides	Orestes	2:00	l. 366	Alas, we look for good on earth...
ELECTRA Sophocles	Orestes	2:30	l. 23	Dearest of servants...
HAMLET Shakespeare	Hamlet	1:15	I v 99	O all you host of heaven!
HAMLET Shakespeare	Hamlet	1:15	I ii 135	O that this too too solid flesh...
HAMLET Shakespeare	Hamlet	1:00	II ii 311	I have of late – but wherefore I know not...
HAMLET Shakespeare	Hamlet	2:00	II ii 555	Now I am alone. O, what a rogue...
HAMLET Shakespeare	Hamlet	1:30	III i 64	To be, or not to be...
HAMLET Shakespeare	Hamlet	1:30	III ii 1	Speak the speech, I pray you...
HAMLET Shakespeare	Hamlet	1:15	III iii 76	Now might I do it pat...
HAMLET Shakespeare	Hamlet	1:30	IV iv 34	How all occasions do inform against me...
HAMLET Shakespeare	Laertes	1:20	I iii 13	Think it no more.
HENRY IV, Pt. 1 Shakespeare	Hal	1:00	I ii 200	I know you all, and will awhile...
HENRY IV, Pt. 1 Shakespeare	Hal	1:15	III ii 132	Do not think so.
HENRY IV, Pt. 1 Shakespeare	Hotspur	1:30	II iii 1	"But, for mine own part, my lord...
HENRY IV, Pt. 1 Shakespeare	Hotspur	2:00	IV iii 59	The King is kind, and well we know...*
HENRY IV, Pt. 2 Shakespeare	Hal	1:45	IV v 152	O, pardon me, my liege!
HENRY IV, Pt. 2 Shakespeare	Hal	1:15	V v 52	I know thee not, old man.
JULIUS CAESAR Shakespeare	Brutus	1:15	II i 10	It must be by his death...
JULIUS CAESAR Shakespeare	Brutus	2:00	III ii 14	Romans, countrymen, and lovers...*
KING LEAR Shakespeare	Edmund	1:20	I ii 1	Thou, Nature, art my goddess...
KING LEAR Shakespeare	Edgar	1:00	II iii 1	I heard myself proclaimed...
MEASURE FOR MEASURE Shakespeare	Angelo	1:15	II ii 201	From thee – even from thy virtue!
MEDEA Euripides	Jason	2:30	l. 522	As for me, it seems I must be...
ORESTES Euripides	Orestes	2:30	l. 270	Get me my horn-tipped bow...

ORESTES Euripides	Orestes	4:00	l. 545	Sir, I shrink from speaking...
PHILOCTETES Sophocles	Odysseus	2:00	l. 56	Ensnare the soul of Philoctetes...
PROMETHEUS BOUND Aeschylus	Prometheus	2:00	l. 89	Bright light, swift-winged winds...
PROMETHEUS BOUND Aeschylus	Prometheus	2:30	l. 199	To speak of this is bitterness.
PROMETHEUS BOUND Aeschylus	Prometheus	3:00	l. 437	Do not think that out of pride...*
RICHARD II Shakespeare	Richard	2:30	V v 1	I have been studying...
ROMEO AND JULIET Shakespeare	Romeo	1:00	II ii 2	But soft! What light through...
ROMEO AND JULIET Shakespeare	Romeo	1:00	III iii 31	'Tis torture, and not mercy.
ROMEO AND JULIET Shakespeare	Romeo	2:00	V iii 74	In faith, I will.
THE TEMPEST Shakespeare	Ariel	1:15	III iii 72	You are three men of sin...

MIDDLE-AGED

AGAMEMNON Aeschylus	Agamemnon	2:30	l. 811	To Argos first, and to the gods within...
ANTONY AND CLEOPATRA - Shakespeare	Antony	1:00	IV viii 1	We have beat him to his camp.
ANTONY AND CLEOPATRA - Shakespeare	Antony	1:15	IV xii 12	All is lost!
CORIOLANUS Shakespeare	Coriolanus	1:30	IV v 72	My name is Caius Marcius, who hath...
HAMLET Shakespeare	King	1:30	I ii 1	Though yet of Hamlet...
HAMLET Shakespeare	King	1:30	III iii 39	O, my offense is rank...
HENRY V Shakespeare	Henry	1:15	III i 1	Once more unto the breach...
HENRY V Shakespeare	Henry	2:15	IV i 234	Upon the King!
HENRY V Shakespeare	Henry	2:00	IV iii 22	What's he that wishes so?
HENRY VI, Pt. 3 Shakespeare	Gloucester	2:00	V vi 66	What, will the aspiring blood...
HENRY VIII Shakespeare	Buckingham	1:30	II i 123	When I came hither...
IPHIGENIA IN AULIS Euripides	Agamemnon	3:00	l. 49	Three girls were born...
JULIUS CAESAR Shakespeare	Antony	1:00	III i 275	O, pardon me thou bleed-ing piece of earth...
JULIUS CAESAR Shakespeare	Antony	4:30	III ii 80	Friends, Romans, countrymen...*
JULIUS CAESAR Shakespeare	Cassius	1:45	I ii 96	I know that virtue to be in you, Brutus...
JULIUS CAESAR Shakespeare	Marullus	1:00	I i 35	Wherefore rejoice? What conquest...
MACBETH Shakespeare	Macbeth	1:30	I vii 1	If it were done when 'tis done...

MACBETH Shakespeare	Macbeth	1:45	II i 42	Is this a dagger which I see before me...
MACBETH Shakespeare	Macbeth	1:00	III i 52	To be thus is nothing...
MEDEA Euripides	Messenger	4:00	l. 1136	When those two children...
OEDIPUS REX Sophocles	Oedipus	2:00	l. 217	For what you ask me...
OEDIPUS REX Sophocles	Oedipus	3:00	l. 771	It shall not be kept from you...
OEDIPUS REX Sophocles	Oedipus	2:00	l. 1370	What I have done here was best done...
OEDIPUS REX Sophocles	Oedipus	2:00	l. 1478	God bless you for it, Creon...
ORESTES Euripides	Menelaus	3:00	l. 682	Believe me, Orestes, I sympathize...
OTHELLO Shakespeare	Othello	1:45	I iii 143	Her father loved me...
OTHELLO Shakespeare	Othello	1:15	III iii 293	This fellow's of exceeding honesty...
OTHELLO Shakespeare	Othello	1:30	V ii 306	Behold, I have a weapon.
OTHELLO Shakespeare	Othello	1:15	V ii 1	It is the cause...
OTHELLO Shakespeare	Iago	1:15	I iii 358	It is merely a lust of the blood...
OTHELLO Shakespeare	Iago	1:00	I iii 401	Thus do I ever make my fool my purse...
OTHELLO Shakespeare	Iago	1:15	II iii 338	And what's he then that says I play the villain...
OTHELLO Shakespeare	Iago	1:15	I i 44	O, sir, content you.
PHILOCTETES Sophocles	Philoctetes	3:00	l. 254	Surely I must be vile!
PHILOCTETES Sophocles	Philoctetes	2:30	l. 927	You fire, you every horror...
PHILOCTETES Sophocles	Philoctetes	2:30	l. 1004	Hands of mine...
RICHARD III Shakespeare	Richard	1:45	I i 1	Now is the winter of our discontent...

OLD

HAMLET Shakespeare	Ghost	1:30	I v 49	Ay, that incestuous, that adulterate beast...
HENRY VIII Shakespeare	Wolsey	1:45	III ii 511	Cromwell, I did not think to shed a tear...
KING LEAR Shakespeare	Lear	1:15	II iv 298	O, reason not the need!
KING LEAR Shakespeare	Lear	1:15	IV vi 123	Ay, every inch a King!
THE MERCHANT OF VENICE - Shakespeare	Shylock	1:00	III i 45	To bait fish withal.
OEDIPUS AT COLONUS Sophocles	Oedipus	1:30	l. 421	Gods! Put not their fires of ambition out!
OEDIPUS AT COLONUS Sophocles	Oedipus	2:30	l. 960	O arrogance unashamed!

ORESTES Euripides	Tyndareus	4:00	I. 491	Understanding, you say?
RICHARD II Shakespeare	Gaunt	1:15	II i 44	This royal throne of kings...
ROMEO AND JULIET Shakespeare	Friar Lawrence	1:45	III iii 118	Hold thy desperate hand.
THE TEMPEST Shakespeare	Prospero	2:30	V i 39	Ye elves of hills, brooks...

CLASSICAL MALE COMIC

YOUNG

THE IMAGINARY INVALID Moliere	Cleante	2:30	II v	Here is the subject of the scene.
LOVE'S LABOUR'S LOST Shakespeare	Berowne	1:15	III i 183	And I, forsooth, in love!
THE MISANTHROPE Moliere	Alceste	1:45	V i	No, you may talk and argue all you can...
MUCH ADO ABOUT NOTHING - Shakespeare	Benedict	1:45	II iii 7	I do much wonder....
MUCH ADO ABOUT NOTHING - Shakespeare	Benedict	1:30	II iii 217	This can be no trick.
ROMEO AND JULIET Shakespeare	Mercutio	1:45	I iv 57	O, then I see Queen Mab...
TWELFTH NIGHT Shakespeare	Sebastian	1:00	IV iii 1	This is the air...
THE WAY OF THE WORLD Congreve	Mirabell	1:30	IV i	Imprimis then, I covenant...*

MIDDLE-AGED

HENRY IV Part 1 Shakespeare	Falstaff	1:45	IV ii 11	If I be not ashamed of my soldiers...
HENRY IV Part 2 Shakespeare	Falstaff	2:00	IV iii 87	I would you had but the wit.
THE IMAGINARY INVALID Moliere	Diaforius	1:45	II v	Sir, it's not because I'm his father...
THE MENAECHMI Plautus	Sponge	1:15	I i	Best way to keep a slave - feed him well.
THE MENAECHMI Plautus	Messenio	1:15	V vi	Beware of beatings...
THE MERRY WIVES OF WINDSOR - Shakespeare	Ford	1:30	II ii 282	What a damned Epicurean rascal is this!
THE MERRY WIVES OF WINDSOR - Shakespeare	Fenton	1:30	IV vi 8	From time to time...
RICHARD III Shakespeare	Richard	1:15	I ii 258	Was ever woman in this humour wooed?
THE SCHOOL FOR WIVES Moliere	Arnolphe	1:15	IV vii	The evil star that's hounding...
THE SCHOOL FOR WIVES Moliere	Chrysalde	2:00	IV viii	It's odd that you, with your good intellect...
THE TAMING OF THE SHREW - Shakespeare	Petruchio	1:00	IV i 186	Thus have I politicly begun my reign...

- 16 -

TARTUFFE Moliere	Tartuffe	1:30	III iii	I may be pious, but I'm human too...
TWELFTH NIGHT Shakespeare	Malvolio	2:15	II v 135	M, O, A, I. This simulation is not...

OLD

AS YOU LIKE IT Shakespeare	Jacques	2:00	II vii 13	A fool, a fool!
AS YOU LIKE IT Shakespeare	Jacques	1:00	II vii 149	All the world's a stage...
HAMLET Shakespeare	Polonius	1:00	I iii 59	Yet here, Laertes?
HAMLET Shakespeare	Polonius	2:00	II ii 92	My liege, and madam, to expostulate...*
LOVE FOR LOVE Congreve	Jeremy	1:15	I i	But sir, is this the way...
THE MISER Moliere	Harpagon	2:00	IV vii	Stop, thief! Stop, thief!
VOLPONE Ben Jonson	Volpone	1:00	I i 70	What should I do...
VOLPONE Ben Jonson	Volpone	2:00	II i 255	No more. Gentlemen, if I had but time...

MODERN MALE SERIOUS

UNDER 20

PLAY Author	CHARACTER (Age)	TIME (approx.)	PLACE	FIRST LINE (Edition Page No.)
FRIENDS Arkady Leokum	The Pupil (12)	2:30	1-act	There's our ship!* (SF 62)
LOVERS (WINNERS) Brian Friel	Joe (17, Irish)	4:30	ep. 2	Mag, there is something I never told you. (Dram 50)
THE QUESTIONING OF NICK – Arthur Kopit – in "The Day the Whores Came Out to Play Tennis..."	Nick (teen-age)	1:30	1-act	That's what ya think, huh?... (H&W 53)

20 - 30

PLAY Author	CHARACTER (Age)	TIME (approx.)	PLACE	FIRST LINE (Edition Page No.)
ALL GOD'S CHILLUN GOT WINGS – Eugene O'Neill – in "Nine Plays"	Jim (20s, Black)	1:15	I, 4	Come. Time we... (RH 110)
BIG TIME BUCK WHITE Joseph Dolan Tuotti	Honey Man (20s, Black)	1:30	1-act	Wow. Look at this... (Grove 2)
BIRDBATH – Leonard Melfi – in "Encounters"	Frankie (late 20s)	1:15	1-act	You see, Velma, most girls...* (RH 26)
BIRDBATH – Leonard Melfi – in "Encounters"	Frankie (late 20s)	1:00	1-act	Her name was Carrie...* (RH 30)
BLUES FOR MISTER CHARLIE James Baldwin	Lorenzo (20, Black)	2:00	I	Well, I wish to God I was in an arsenal.* (Dell 15)
CALL ME BY MY RIGHTFUL NAME – Michael Shurtleff	Paul (27, Black)	3:15	II, 2	I've never told anyone... (DPS 44)
CAMELOT (MUSICAL) Alan Jay Lerner	Arthur (25, English)	1:30	I, 11	Proposition: If I could choose... (Dell 215)
CEREMONIES IN DARK OLD MEN – Lonne Elder III	Blue (20s, Black)	2:00	II, 1	The other day, I went up... (SF 69)
THE CHERRY ORCHARD Anton Chekhov	Trofimoff (27)	1:15	II	Humanity goes forward... (SF 43)
DUTCHMAN LeRoi Jones	Clay (20, Black)	4:30	sc. 2	I'm not telling you again... (Morrow 34)
EQUUS Peter Shaffer	Alan (21, English)	2:15	sc. 13	I was pushed forward... (Deutsch 47)
EVENTS WHILE GUARDING THE BOFORS GUN John McGrath	O'Rourke (29, Irish)	2:00	II, 2	The Bofors gun, sirs... (Methuen 82)
FERRYBOAT – Leonard Melfi – in "Encounters"	Joey (28)	1:45	1-act	Yeah. Long time ago.* (RH 125)
FERRYBOAT – Leonard Melfi – in "Encounters"	Joey (28)	1:30	1-act	Well, I go there a lot... (RH 129)
FIVE FINGER EXERCISE Peter Shaffer	Walter (20, German)	1:30	II, 2	Clive? What's the matter? (SFL 68)
THE FREEDOM OF THE CITY – Brian Friel	Michael (22, Irish)	1:00	II	We came out... (Faber 71)
FUNNYHOUSE OF A NEGRO – Adrienne Kennedy	Man (20s, Black)	3:00	1-act	I always dreamed of a day... (SF 16)
THE GLASS MENAGERIE Tennessee Williams	Tom (22)	2:00	I, 1	I have tricks in my pocket... (DPS 11)
THE GLASS MENAGERIE Tennessee Williams	Tom (22)	1:45	II, 7	And so the following evening I... (DPS 41)

Play / Author	Character	Time	Act/Scene	Line
THE GLASS MENAGERIE Tennessee Williams	Jim (25)	2:00	II, 8	Say! You know what I judge...* (DPS 59)
THE GLASS MENAGERIE Tennessee Williams	Tom (22)	1:15	II, 8	I didn't go to the moon. (DPS 68)
HADRIAN THE SEVENTH Peter Luke	Fr. Rose (29)	1:45	II, 7	Prosit Quaesumus, Domine... (SF 78)
THE HAIRY APE Eugene O'Neill	Yank (20s)	2:30	sc. 1	Aw, take it easy. Yuh're aw right... (RH 175)
THE HAIRY APE Eugene O'Neill	Yank (20s)	4:30	sc. 8	Welcome to your city, huh? (RH 228)
HALLOWEEN – Leonard Melfi – in "Encounters"	Luke (29)	3:15	1-act	Margaret...you know, you really... (RH 112)
HELLO AND GOODBYE Athol Fugard	Johnny (20s, White South African)	4:30	I	Three fifty-five, three fifty-six... (SF 5)
INDIANS Arthur Kopit	John Grass (20s, Indian)	1:15	sc. 2	Brothers! I am going to talk... (H&W 9)
THE KITCHEN Arnold Wesker	Paul (20s, Jewish)	2:00	(interlude)	Listen, I'll tell you something. (Cape 57)
LAZARUS LAUGHED Eugene O'Neill – in "Nine Plays"	Caligula (21)	2:45	IV, 2	Hail, Caligula! (RH 479)
LEMON SKY Lanford Wilson	Alan (29, mid-Westerner)	2:00	I	I've been trying to tell this story... (DPS 7)
THE LION AND THE JEWEL Wole Soyinka	Lakunle (23, Black)	1:15	night	Within a year or two, I swear... (Oxford 36)
LONG DAY'S JOURNEY INTO NIGHT – Eugene O'Neill	Edmund (23)	1:30	IV	To hell with sense! (Yale 130)
LONG DAY'S JOURNEY INTO NIGHT – Eugene O'Neill	Edmund (23)	1:00	IV	God, Papa, ever since I went to sea... (Yale 145)
LONG DAY'S JOURNEY INTO NIGHT – Eugene O'Neill	Edmund (23)	2:30	IV	For Christ's sake, Papa, forget it! (Yale 152)
LOOK BACK IN ANGER John Osborne	Jimmy (25, English)	1:30	I	Oh, my dear wife... (Dram 30)
LOOK BACK IN ANGER John Osborne	Jimmy (25, English)	1:30	II, 1	Anyone who's never watched... (Dram 46)
A MURDER HAS BEEN ARRANGED – Emlyn Williams	Mullins (20s, English)	1:30	II	I've studied myself for years... (SF 55)
NIGHT MUST FALL Emlyn Williams	Dan (20s, Welsh)	1:15	III, 2	You didn't ought to read so much.* (SF 136)
PHILADELPHIA, HERE I COME! – Brian Friel	Gar (Private) (20s, Irish)	1:45	III, 1	When you're curled up in your wee cot... (SF 65)
THE PICTURE OF DORIAN GRAY – John Osborne	Dorian (20s, English)	3:45	III, 1	Mysticism. How fairly... (Faber 73)
THE RULING CLASS Peter Barnes	Earl of Gurney (20s, English)	1:30	II, 4	Deformed, unfinished, sent before... (Grove 86)
SAVAGES Christopher Hampton	Carlos (20s, Brazilian)	2:00	sc. 13	Listen, I won't go...* (Faber 66)
THE SEA GULL Anton Chekhov	Trepleff (25)	2:45	I	She's set against me... (SF 6)
THE SHIRT – Leonard Melfi – in "Encounters"	Clarence (20s, Southern)	3:00	1-act	Ain't that a bitch? (RH 162)
THE SHIRT – Leonard Melfi – in "Encounters"	Clarence (20s, Southern)	6:00	1-act	Shiiiiittt! You ain't really...* (RH 165)
THE SIGN IN SIDNEY BRUSTEIN'S WINDOW Lorraine Hansberry	Alton (27, Black)	1:30	II, 3	My father, you know, he was... (SF 84)
STRANGE INTERLUDE Eugene O'Neill – in "Three Plays"	Evans (26)	2:30	Pt. 1, Act IV	No use...can't think of... (RH 114)

SUMMERTREE Ron Cowen	Young Man (20)	1:45	I	It's hot out here, just sitting... (DPS 5)
SWEET EROS Terrence McNally	Young Man (20s)	1:30	sc. 3	So I suppose it was inevitable. (DPS 10)
TIMES SQUARE – Leonard Melfi – in "Encounters"	Mr. Fascination (under 25)	2:15	1-act	Why did you have to go... (RH 203)
THE TRIAL OF THE CATONSVILLE 9 Daniel Berrigan	Thomas Lewis (28)	1:00	–	There was a difference in our... (SF 28)
THE WARM PENINSULA Joe Masteroff	Steve (late 20s)	1:00	II	One afternoon I took Mickey... (SF 60)
WATERCOLOR Philip Magdalany	Andrew (20s)	1:30	1-act	I just sat on the beach... (DPS 49)
WELCOME TO ANDROMEDA Ron Whyte	Boy (21)	1:30	1-act	Anyway, those are my... (SF 25)
THE WHITE LIARS Peter Shaffer	Tom (20s, English)	5·00	1-act	If I had the gift... (SF 34)

30 - 40

ALFIE Bill Naughton	Alfie (30s, Cockney)	2:30	III, 1	I didn't like goin' off... (SFL 60)
ALPHA BETA E.A. Whitehead	Mr. Elliot (30s, English)	2:30	III	Go on...tell me... (Faber 58)
THE BARRETTS OF WIMPOLE STREET – Rudolf Besier	Browning (30s, English)	2:00	II	Oh, very well – then I'll say nothing.* (DPS 54)
BECKET Jean Anouilh	Henry (30s, English)	1:30	I, 1	If you think I'm in the mood... (SFL 2)
BECKET Jean Anouilh	Becket (30s, English)	1:15	II, 4	I must say it was all very pretty stuff. (SFL 41)
BECKET Jean Anouilh	Becket (30s, English)	2:30	III, 6	Yet, it would be simple enough. (SFL 57)
THE BIG KNIFE Clifford Odets	Charlie (30s)	1:30	II	No, let me talk – don't push me back... (DPS 49)
BIG TIME BUCK WHITE Joseph Dolan Tuotti	Big Time (30, Black)	1:30	1-act	Now, that's the thing... (Grove 99)
BIG TIME BUCK WHITE Joseph Dolan Tuotti	Big Time (30, Black)	1:45	1-act	Whether or not we're going... (Grove 104)
THE BLOOD KNOT Athol Fugard	Morris (30, White South African)	4:00	sc. 1	We are brothers, remember. (SF 23)
THE BLOOD KNOT Athol Fugard	Zachariah (30, Black South African)	2:30	sc. 6	Ma. Ma! Mother! (SF 88)
BLUES FOR MISTER CHARLIE James Baldwin	Parnell (30)	2:15	III	She says I called somebody... (Dell 139)
THE BOYS IN THE BAND Mart Crowley	Michael (30)	1:15	I	Oh, you know it all by heart anyway. (SF 13)
CAMINO REAL Tennessee Williams	Kilroy (30s)	1:15	Block 3	That is very peculiar. (DPS 27)
CAMINO REAL Tennessee Williams	Lord Byron (30)	1:15	Block 8	When Shelley's corpse was recovered... (DPS 53)
THE CARETAKER Harold Pinter	Aston (early 30s, English)	4:15	II, 3	I used to go there quite a bit. (DPS 41)
CAT ON A HOT TIN ROOF Tennessee Williams	Brick (30, Southern)	1:30	II	All right. You're askin' for it...* (DPS 57)
THE CHERRY ORCHARD Anton Chekhov	Lopahin (30s)	2:00	III	I bought it. I bought it. (SF 69)
CYRANO DE BERGERAC Edmond Rostand	Cyrano (30)	2:30	II	What would you have me do? (Bantam 75)

Title & Author	Character	Time	Act/Scene	Opening Line & Source
DARK VICTORY – George Brewer & Bertram Bloch	Dr. Steele (35-40)	1:45	I	I was a farmer's son in this same town... (DPS 20)
THE DEVILS John Whiting	Grandier (35)	3:00	II	I've been out of the town.* (H &W 96)
DYLAN Sidney Michaels	Dylan (39, Welsh)	2:30	I	I've no time to think about...* (SF 16)
DYLAN Sidney Michaels	Dylan (39, Welsh)	2:00	II	I'm me. I smoke too much. (SF 76)
THE EXERCISE Lewis John Carlino	The Actor (30s)	1:30	I	Glib. Glib from the crib. (DPS 13)
THE FANTASTICKS (MUSICAL) – Tom Jones & Harvey Schmidt	El Gallo (35)	1:15	I	You wonder how these things begin. (Avon 54)
FLOWERS FOR ALGERNON David Rogers	Charlie (30s)	1:00	II	September twenty-first. (Dram 109)
HOGAN'S GOAT William Alfred	Stanton (30s)	1:45	I, 1	Are you the only exile of us all? (SF 13)
INADMISSIBLE EVIDENCE John Osborne	Bill (39, English)	6:00	I	Please forgive me.* (Dram 13)
INADMISSIBLE EVIDENCE John Osborne	Bill (39, English)	7:00	II	Get me another glass of water. (Dram 127)
INDIANS Arthur Kopit	Buffalo Bill (30s)	1:45	sc. 11	Well, as you've just seen... (H &W 68)
IN WHITE AMERICA Martin Duberman	Nat Turner (35, Black)	1:30	I	I was thirty-five years of age... (SF 25)
JOE EGG Peter Nichols	Bri (33, English)	4:00	II	Sheila and I went with her... (Grove 83)
LONG DAY'S JOURNEY INTO NIGHT – Eugene O'Neill	Jamie (33)	1:00	IV	Don't be a dumbbell! (Yale 163)
LUTHER John Osborne	Luther (30s)	4:00	II, 3	My text is from the Epistle of Paul... (Dram 55)
LUTHER John Osborne	Luther (30s)	1:30	II, 6	I have been served... (Dram 71)
MISS JULIE August Strindberg	Jean (30)	2:45	1-act	Do you know what the world...* (Avon 39)
NIGHT LIFE Sidney Kingsley	Neil (30s)	2:00	I	Yes. There were many voices... (DPS 8)
OBJECTIVE CASE Lewis John Carlino	He (30)	1:30	1-act	There are two of me. (DPS 48)
THE PETRIFIED FOREST Robert Sherwood	Squier (35)	1:15	II	This insurance policy... (DPS 55)
THE PHILANTHROPIST Christopher Hampton	Philip (30, English)	1:45	sc. 5	I'll tell you something... (SF 60)
POOR BITOS Jean Anouilh	Bitos (30s)	1:15	I	I tried with all my might to be your friend.* (SFL 19)
A RAISIN IN THE SUN Lorraine Hansberry	Walter (30s, Black)	2:00	III	Where is the bottom?* (SF 98)
RIDE A COCK HORSE David Mercer	Peter (30)	2:00	II, 1	Can you hear those insects? (H &W 72)
THE SEA GULL Anton Chekhov	Trigorin (30s)	3:45	II	I don't see anything so very beautiful...* (SF 28)
STRANGE INTERLUDE Eugene O'Neill – in "Three Plays of Eugene O'Neill"	Marsden (35)	2:30	Pt. 1, Act I	How perfectly the Professor's... (RH 62)
STRANGE INTERLUDE Eugene O'Neill – in "Three Plays of Eugene O'Neill"	Marsden (35)	2:00	Pt. 1, Act II	Prophetic Professor!...I remember he... (RH 78)

Title / Author	Character	Time	Act/Scene	Cue
SWEET BIRD OF YOUTH Tennessee Williams	Chance (30s)	4:30	I, 2	Here is the town I was born in...* (DPS 28)
TALK TO ME LIKE THE RAIN AND LET ME LISTEN Tennessee Williams - in "27 Wagons Full of Cotton"	Man (30)	2:30	1-act	When I woke up I was in a bathtub...* (ND 213)
THE TIME OF YOUR LIFE William Saroyan	Krupp (37)	3:00	IV	The strike isn't enough...* (SF 133)
TWO FOR THE SEESAW William Gibson	Jerry (30s)	1:30	II, 3	All these months I've been... (SF 66)

40 - 60

Title / Author	Character	Time	Act/Scene	Cue
ABE LINCOLN IN ILLINOIS Robert E. Sherwood	Abe (50s)	5:00	III, 9	Judge Douglas has paid tribute... (DPS 61)
ABE LINCOLN IN ILLINOIS Robert E. Sherwood	Abe (50s)	2:00	III, 12	No one, not in my situation... (DPS 81)
THE ADDING MACHINE Elmer L. Rice	Zero (50)	7:00	sc. 4	Sure I killed him. (SF 51)
ANTIGONE Jean Anouilh	Creon (50)	2:15	-	Oedipus was too chicken-hearted... (SF 55)
BLOOD, SWEAT AND STANLEY POOLE - James & William Goldman	Poole (47)	1:30	II, 3	It doesn't matter. Not really. (DPS 56)
BLUES FOR MISTER CHARLIE James Baldwin	Meridian (40s, Black)	3:00	II	My heart is heavier... (Dell 103)
THE BURIAL OF ESPOSITO Ronald Ribman - in "Passing Through from Exotic Places"	Nick (late 40s, Italian)	3:15	1-act	You want to hear something? (DPS 67)
A CASE OF LIBEL Henry Denker	Sloane (middle 40s)	4:45	III	May it please the Court... (SF 86)
CEREMONIES IN DARK OLD MEN - Lonne Elder III	Parker (50s, Black)	3:00	II, 2	"Mr. Parker." Call me champ! (SF 84)
CHILDREN OF THE WIND Jerry Devine	Brophy (40s)	2:00	III, 2	Don't give me that... (DPS 50)
CHILD'S PLAY Robert Marasco	Malley (40s)	1:15	I	I had a Christmas card... (SF 41)
THE EMPEROR JONES Eugene O'Neill	Jones (middle-age, Black)	4:00	sc. 2	Well, heah I is. (ACC 30)
THE EMPEROR JONES Eugene O'Neill	Jones (middle-age, Black)	3:00	sc. 4	I'm meltin' wid heat! (ACC 37)
EMPEROR OF HAITI Langston Hughes - in "Black Drama in America: an Anthology"	Dessalines (40s, Black)	2:00	II, 2	Drums in the court!* (Fawcett 96)
ENDGAME Samuel Beckett	Hamm (middle-age)	4:30	1-act	One! Silence! Where was I? (Grove 50)
THE ENTERTAINER John Osborne	Archie (50, English)	4:15	sc. 8	No, stay up for a while.* (Dram 73)
THE ENTERTAINER John Osborne	Archie (50, English)	3:45	sc. 13	We're all out for good old... (Dram 92)
EQUUS Peter Shaffer	Dysart (40s, English)	3:45	sc. 35	All right! I'll take... (Deutsch 105)
FATHER UXBRIDGE WANTS TO MARRY - Frank Gagliano	Morden (40s)	3:45	1-act	How can I kill her with... (DPS 33)
HADRIAN THE SEVENTH Peter Luke	Rolfe (40s, English)	1:00	I, 1	You can't get shit from a wooden... (SF 11)
HADRIAN THE SEVENTH Peter Luke	Hadrian (40s, English)	1:45	II, 2	You wish to denounce Us... (SF 45)

HADRIAN THE SEVENTH Peter Luke	Hadrian (40s, English)	4:00	II, 6	Pseudonyms: when I was kicked out...* (SF 65)
I NEVER SANG FOR MY FATHER - Robert Anderson	Gene (40)	1:15	II	That night I left my Father's... (DPS 62)
INADMISSIBLE EVIDENCE John Osborne	Maples (40, English)	5:00	II	My name is John Montague...* (Dram 118)
INQUEST Donald Freed	Bloch (50)	1:15	I	What I would like to impress... (SF 15)
THE INVESTIGATION Peter Weiss	5th Witness (middle-age)	1:30	(Song of the Camp)	Even as I jumped out of the... (Dram 47)
IN WHITE AMERICA Martin Duberman	Jefferson (40s)	1:15	I	The love of justice and the love... (SF 14)
THE LONG VOYAGE HOME Eugene O'Neill - in "Seven Plays of the Sea"	Olson (40s, Swedish)	1:15	1-act	You know, Miss Freda... (RH 72)
LOVERS (LOSERS) Brian Friel	Andy (50, Irish)	1:45	sc. 3	I don't think I told you... (Dram 113)
LUTHER John Osborne	Tetzel (middle-age)	5:30	II, 1	Are you wondering who I am... (Dram 43)
LUTHER John Osborne	Knight (middle-age)	3:30	III, 2	There was excitement that day. (Dram 78)
LUTHER John Osborne	Luther (40s)	1:30	III, 2	Christ! Hear Me! (Dram 82)
THE MADNESS OF LADY BRIGHT - Lanford Wilson - in "The Rimers of Eldritch..."	Leslie (40)	3:00	1-act	Oh, not good. Not good at all.* (H&W 79)
THE MAN IN THE GLASS BOOTH - Robert Shaw	Goldman (52, Jewish)	3:45	II	Excuse me, Your Honor.* (SF 52)
MIDDLE OF THE NIGHT Paddy Chayefsky	Manufacturer (53)	2:00	II, 2	He called his wife from...* (SF 40)
A MOON FOR THE MISBEGOTTEN - Eugene O'Neill	Tyrone (40s)	6:00	III	When Mama died...* (RH 94)
MURDER IN THE CATHEDRAL T.S. Eliot	Archbishop (40, English)	3:30	(interlude)	Dear children of God... (HB 47)
REBECCA Daphne Du Maurier	Maxim (middle-age)	3:00	II, 3	How could I tell you?* (DPS 51)
ROYAL HUNT OF THE SUN Peter Shaffer	Old Martin (50s)	1:30	I, 1	Save you all. My name is Martin. (SF 13)
ROYAL HUNT OF THE SUN Peter Shaffer	Old Martin (50s)	1:15	I, 8	Have you ever climbed a mountain... (SF 40)
SAVAGES Christopher Hampton	West (50s, English)	2:00	sc. 1	Origin of fire. (Faber 23)
SAVAGES Christopher Hampton	Penn (50s, English)	2:30	sc. 11	Well, Alan, I've... (Faber 55)
SERJEANT MUSGRAVE'S DANCE - John Arden	Musgrave (40, English)	2:30	III, 1	Now there's more tales than one...* (Grove 80)
SILENT NIGHT, LONELY NIGHT - Robert Anderson	John (early 40s)	1:30	I, 1	It was just before Christmas. (SF 18)
THE SLAVE LeRoi Jones	Walker (40, Black)	1:45	1-act	OK. OK. However you want it... (Morrow 66)
TIGER AT THE GATES Jean Giraudoux	Ulysses (40s)	1:30	II	It's usual on the eve... (SF 65)
TINY ALICE Edward Albee	Julian (middle-age)	6:00	III	Goodbye, dear Julian. (DPS 93)
TO KILL A MOCKINGBIRD Christopher Sergel	Atticus (50)	2:30	II	Gentlemen, this case is not...* (Dram 144)

THE TRIAL OF THE CATONSVILLE 9 Daniel Berrigan	Daniel (49)	1:45	–	On a June morning, I lay before... (SF 5)
THE TRIAL OF THE CATONSVILLE 9 Daniel Berrigan	Philip (47)	1:00	–	Yes, we violated the law... (SF 33)
THE TRIAL OF THE CATONSVILLE 9 Daniel Berrigan	Daniel (49)	2:00	–	Our apologies, good friends... (SF 38)
THE TRIAL OF THE CATONSVILLE 9 Daniel Berrigan	Prosecution (middle–age)	2:15	–	The government is ready... (SF 40)
THE TRIAL OF THE CATONSVILLE 9 Daniel Berrigan	Defense (middle–age)	2:00	–	Ladies and gentlemen of the jury. (SF 41)
TWELVE ANGRY MEN Sherman L. Sergel	Ten (40s)	1:00	III	I don't understand you people. (Dram 59)
UNDER MILK WOOD Dylan Thomas	1st Voice (any age)	2:30	1–act	To begin at the beginning... (ND 1)
A VIEW FROM THE BRIDGE Arthur Miller	Alfieri (50s, Italian)	1:45	I	You wouldn't have known it... (DPS 6)
VIVAT! VIVAT REGINA! Robert Bolt	Knox (middle–age, Scot)	2:00	I, 2	Welcome to Scotland. (SFL 9)
WAITING FOR GODOT Samuel Beckett	Vladimir (middle–age)	2:00	II	Let us not waste...* (Grove 51)
WHO'S AFRAID OF VIRGINIA WOOLF? Edward Albee	George (46)	1:45	II	When I was sixteen and going to... (DPS 46)

60 AND OVER

THE CARETAKER Harold Pinter	Davies (old, English)	2:15	III, 2	What do you expect me to do? (DPS 51)
DEATH OF A SALESMAN Arthur Miller	Willy (60)	1:30	II	Oh, yeah, my father lived... (DPS 58)
DESIRE UNDER THE ELMS Eugene O'Neill – in "Three Plays of Eugene O'Neill"	Cabot (75)	2:45	II, 2	Will ye ever know me... (RH 31)
ENDGAME Samuel Beckett	Nagg (old)	1:30	1–act	Let me tell it again. (Grove 22)
THE ENTERTAINER John Osborne	Billy (70, English)	1:20	sc. 10	Oh, Charlie should be all right. (Dram 86)
FLINT David Mercer	Flint (70, English)	2:00	II, 1	Dixie – no. But how can you... (Methuen 53)
GALILEO Bertolt Brecht	Galileo (old)	3:00	sc. 13	No? My dear Sarti... (Grove 123)
THE HAIRY APE Eugene O'Neill	Paddy (old, Irish)	1:30	sc. 1	We belong to this, you're... (RH 173)
HOGAN'S GOAT William Alfred	Quinn (70s, Irish–Am)	1:30	I, 4	You heard me, James. (SF 39)
INDIANS Arthur Kopit	Joseph (very old, Indian)	1:45	sc. 9	In the moon of the cherries... (H&W 55)
I NEVER SANG FOR MY FATHER – Robert Anderson	Tom (80)	2:30	I	I was downstairs in the kitchen...* (DPS 25)
INHERIT THE WIND Jerome Lawrence & Robert E. Lee	Drummond (60s)	1:30	III	Some day I'm going to get me...* (DPS 75)

THE LAST OF MY SOLID GOLD WATCHES - Tennessee Williams - in "27 Wagons Full of Cotton"	Charlie (78)	1:30	1-act	I just want you to know... (ND 83)
THE LION AND THE JEWEL Wole Soyinka	Baroka (62, Black)	2:00	(Noon)	I wanted Sidi because I...* (Oxford 29)
LONG DAY'S JOURNEY INTO NIGHT Eugene O'Neill	Tyrone (65, Irish-Am)	1:30	IV	More morbidness! (Yale 147)
LONG DAY'S JOURNEY INTO NIGHT Eugene O'Neill	Tyrone (65, Irish-Am)	2:00	IV	Yes, maybe life overdid the lesson... (Yale 149)
MARAT/SADE Peter Weiss	Sade (68)	2:00	I, 12	Correct Marat... (Pocket Book 42)
THE ROYAL HUNT OF THE SUN - Peter Shaffer	Pizarro (60s)	1:15	I, 7	Stand firm. Firmer!... (SF 37)
THE ROYAL HUNT OF THE SUN - Peter Shaffer	Pizarro (60s)	3:00	II, 7	Leave it now. There's no cure... (SF 81)
THE ROYAL HUNT OF THE SUN - Peter Shaffer	Pizarro (60s)	2:00	II, 12	Cheat! You've cheated me! (SF 98)
SCRATCH Archibald MacLeish	Webster (60s)	6:00	4	The question for the jury, sir? (Dram 73)
THE SLAVE LeRoi Jones	Walker (old, Black)	3:30	(prologue)	Whatever the core of our lives. (Morrow 43)
SLOW DANCE ON THE KILLING GROUND William Hanley	Glas (65, German)	3:00	II, 2	But I had a wife who was a Jew. (DPS 55)
SWAN SONG - Anton Chekhov - in "The Brute and Other Farces"	Svetlovidov (68, Russian)	2:30	1-act	When I was a young actor...* (SF 14)

MODERN MALE COMIC

UNDER 20

BILLY LIAR - Waterhouse & Hall	Billy (19)	1:30	I	The Fisher residence? (SF 34)
THE HOUSE OF BLUE LEAVES - John Guare	Ronnie (18)	3:00	II, 1	My father tell you all about me? (SF 35)
LOVERS (WINNERS) Brian Friel	Joe (17, Irish)	2:15	episode 2	We're about 450 feet above sea... (Dram 60)
THE MOUSE THAT ROARED Christopher Sergel	Page (young)	1:00	I	To the President, Congress... (Dram 21)
YOU'RE A GOOD MAN, CHARLIE BROWN (MUSICAL) - Clark Gesner	Charlie Brown (8)	2:30	I	I think lunchtime is about... (Fawcett 23)
YOU'RE A GOOD MAN, CHARLIE BROWN (MUSICAL) - Clark Gesner	Snoopy (an ageless dog)	1:45	II	Here's the World War One flying ace... (Fawcett 69)

20 - 30

BRINGING IT ALL BACK HOME - Terrence McNally	Jimmy (20)	1:45	1-act	Well here's Jimmy. (DPS 32)

THE CARETAKER Harold Pinter	Mick (late 20s, English)	2:00	II, 1	You're stinking the place out. (DPS 27)
FIVE ON THE BLACK HAND SIDE – Charlie L. Russell	Fun Loving (20s, Black)	1:45	II	In my alley, if you're hip... (SF 49)
FLINT David Mercer	Swash (late 20s, English)	1:45	I, 1	Faith is the substance of things... (Methuen 7)
HAIL SCRAWDYKE! David Halliwell	Scrawdyke (25, North Country English)	1:45	sc. 5	Friends. Fellow fighters. People... (Grove 80)
HOME FIRES John Guare	Rudy (25)	2:30	1-act	I personally represent the Ben Hur...* (SF 55)
IT'S CALLED THE SUGAR PLUM – Israel Horovitz	Zuckerman (22, Jewish)	1:30	1-act	You know what the most beautiful...* (DPS 25)
THE KNACK Ann Jellicoe	Tolen (20s, English)	1:45	I	You mean how I get women?* (SF 26)
LOVERS AND OTHER STRANGERS – Taylor & Bologna	Mike (20s)	2:30	3	We already talked. What do you expect... (SF 24)
LUNCHTIME – Leonard Melfi – in "Encounters"	Rex (27)	1:45	1-act	Well, anyway, I was going...* (RH 49)
THE MATCHMAKER Thornton Wilder	Cornelius (20)	1:45	II	Isn't the world full of wonderful things? (SF 47)
THE NATIONAL HEALTH OR NURSE NORTON'S AFFAIR – Peter Nichols	Barnet (20s, English)	2:15	I, 10	A woman's work is never done. (SF 48)
NEXT TIME I'LL SING TO YOU – James Saunders	Meff (20s)	1:45	I	Think of all the great lives... (DPS 31)
NOURISH THE BEAST Steve Tesich	Criminal (20, Oriental)	1:15	I, 4	Hey...Hey... (SF 31)
THE OFAY WATCHER Frank Cucci	Rufus (20s, Black)	1:45	3	I know how to act.* (DPS 22)
OH DAD, POOR DAD, MAMMA'S HUNG YOU IN THE CLOSET AND I'M FEELIN' SO SAD – Arthur Kopit	Jonathan (20)	2:15	sc. 2	Well, I made it out of lenses and tubing. (SF 19)
THE PAISLEY CONVERTIBLE Harry Cauley	Charlie (late 20s)	1:30	III	Amy? Amy? Come out... (SF 50)
PLAY IT AGAIN, SAM Woody Allen	Allan (29)	1:30	II	Mildred Denberg...can't even remember... (SF 27)
ROMANOFF AND JULIET Peter Ustinov	Igor (20s, Russian)	1:45	II	Theory is a corset. (DPS 36)
THE STAR-SPANGLED GIRL Neil Simon	Andy (26)	1:15	I, 1	Fallout magazine...Who's calling... (DPS 8)
SUNSTROKE – Ronald Ribman – in "Passing Through from Exotic Places"	Arthur (20, Jewish)	2:30	1-act	No, I'm all right. I don't even...* (DPS 42)
TIMES SQUARE – Leonard Melfi – in "Encounters"	Butch (under 25)	1:30	1-act	It's getting late. (RH 194)
THE TYPISTS Murray Schisgal	Paul (20s)	1:30	1-act	I was born in a poor section... (DPS 12)
WITNESS Terrence McNally	Young Man	2:45	1-act	A word about motivation... (DPS 45)

ANY AGE

From BEYOND THE FRINGE Bennett – Cook – Miller – Moore Man Bites Dog		1:30	I	Good, good! Good God!* (SF 11)

From BEYOND THE FRINGE Bennett - Cook - Miller - Moore				
Fruits of Experience		3:30	I	We're going to have just a little chat... (SF 13)
The Heat Death of the Universe		3:00	I	Some years ago, when I was rather... (SF 16)
Porn Shopping		2:30	II	Some years ago when I was... (SF 40)
Take a Pew		2:45	II	The eleventh verse of the... (SF 49)
The English Way of Death (Cockney)		3:00	"64"	I'm just having a look for... (SF 63)
Death of Lord Nelson		1:30	"64"	One of the strangest episodes... (SF 73)
The Miner		5:00	"64"	Yes, I could have been a judge... (SF 77)
FEIFFER'S PEOPLE Jules Feiffer	Man	1:00	-	As part of a fact-finding... (DPS 22)
MIXED DOUBLES George Melly	Bank Manager	2:00	1-act	If it was up to me... (Methuen 20)
SCENES FROM AMERICAN LIFE - A.R. Gurney, Jr.	Minister	1:00	I	The Gospel for today is... (SF 16)

30 - 40

ADAPTATION Elaine May	Father (30s)	1:00	1-act	Not yet. As a... (DPS 6)
ALFIE Bill Naughton	Alfie (30s, Cockney)	2:30	II, 1	'Ere, once you know you... (SFL 27)
COP-OUT John Guare	Policeman (30s)	3:00	1-act	When I was a kid... (SF 6)
CRAWLING ARNOLD Jules Feiffer	Arnold (early 30s)	1:45	1-act	Well, in a fantasy, it's you... (DPS 17)
CRITIC'S CHOICE Ira Levin	Parker (late 30s)	1:15	III	Angie, I cannot and will not... (DPS 67)
A DAY FOR SURPRISES John Guare	Mr. Falanzano (30s)	5:00	1-act	Books...poets...Alfred Lord Tennyson. (DPS 19)
THE HOMECOMING Harold Pinter	Lenny (30s, English)	2:00	I	I mean, I am very sensitive... (Grove 32)
INFANCY Thornton Wilder	Avonzino (30s)	1:30	1-act	Wednesday, April 26... Right... (SF 5)
THE JOURNEY OF THE FIFTH HORSE - Ronald Ribman	Zoditch (35)	1:45	II	Let the house freeze... (SF 43)
THE JOURNEY OF THE FIFTH HORSE - Ronald Ribman	Zoditch (35)	1:15	II	Too old? I am... (SF 75)
LITTLE MURDERS Jules Feiffer	Dupas (30)	5:30	I, 3	You all know why we're here. (SF 38)
LITTLE MURDERS Jules Feiffer	Alfred (30)	3:00	II, 1	During Korea - I was in college... (SF 45)
LITTLE MURDERS Jules Feiffer	Practice (35)	4:00	II, 2	I needed this. (SF 57)
A MARRIAGE PROPOSAL Anton Chekhov	Lomov (30s)	1:00	1-act	I'm cold. My whole body... (SF 6)
OH, MEN! OH, WOMEN! Edward Chodorov	Arthur (30s)	4:00	II	Silence, goddammit, I'm on! (SF 59)

Play / Author	Character	Time	Act/Scene	Opening Line
THE PHILANTHROPIST Christopher Hampton	Braham (30s, English)	2:00	sc. 3	My dear chap, what I think...* (SF 22)
THE PHILANTHROPIST Christopher Hampton	Don (30, English)	3:00	sc. 3	Very sad case, was Boot.* (SF 25)
THE PHILANTHROPIST Christopher Hampton	Don (30, English)	2:30	sc. 6	Oh, I live by a lie.* (SF 65)
THE PUBLIC EYE Peter Shaffer	Cristoforou (30s, English)	1:30	1-act	Briefly, then, I am a middleman. (SF 37)
PURLIE VICTORIOUS Ossie Davis	Purlie (30s, Black)	1:45	(Epilogue)	And toll the bell, Big Bethel...* (SF 81)
READY WHEN YOU ARE, C.B.! - Susan Slade	Jonas (30)	1:00	II, 2	About the famous movie director... (SF 60)
ROSENCRANTZ AND GUILDENSTERN ARE DEAD Tom Stoppard	Rosencrantz (30, English)	3:00	II	Do you ever think of yourself as...* (SF 54)
SCUBA DUBA Bruce Jay Friedman	Harold (35)	3:45	I	That's the whole Juan story? (DPS 18)
SCUBA DUBA Bruce Jay Friedman	Harold (35)	1:45	I	Well, first I thought I'd...* (DPS 21)
SCUBA DUBA Bruce Jay Friedman	Harold (35)	3:15	I	I'll tell you what it's like. (DPS 27)
STEAMBATH Bruce Jay Friedman	Attendant (30s, Puerto Rican)	2:30	I	Hiya, Baby. San Diego Freeway...* (SF 20)
A THOUSAND CLOWNS Herb Gardner	Murray (middle 30s)	2:00	I	Well, see, last week... (SF 13)
A THOUSAND CLOWNS Herb Gardner	Murray (middle 30s)	1:30	I	For five years she did everything... (SF 28)
WHO'S HAPPY NOW? Oliver Hailey	Richard (30)	1:30	I	My mother's here tonight. (DPS 5)
WITNESS Terrence McNally	Window Washer (30s)	2:45	1-act	I'm gonna write a book someday. (DPS 35)

40 - 60

Play / Author	Character	Time	Act/Scene	Opening Line
THE BRUTE Anton Chekhov	Smirnov (middle- age, Russian)	2:15	1-act	"Now you're being silly..." (SF 31)
CELIMARE Labiche & Delacour	Celimare (47, French)	2:00	I	This is my little box of... (H&W 59)
COME LIVE WITH ME Minoff & Price	Rademacher (50)	1:15	II	I got no secrets.* (SF 41)
DAY OF ABSENCE Douglas Turner Ward	Mayor (middle- age, Black)	4:45	1-act	Jackson, re-grease the machinery...* (DPS 53)
THE DAY THE WHORES CAME OUT TO PLAY TENNIS - Arthur Kopit	Franklin (47)	2:30	1-act	Hello. You still there?* (H&W 102)
DEAR LIAR Jerome Kilty	Shaw (40s, English)	2:00	II	Then seven years passed... (SF 48)
THE GOOD DOCTOR Neil Simon	Peter (middle-age)	1:45	I, 6	If I may say so... (RH 47)
THE GOOD DOCTOR Neil Simon	Writer (40s)	1:30	II, 1	Just getting a little... (RH 67)
HABEAS CORPUS Alan Bennett	Wicksteed (53, English)	1:30	I	In the course of...* (Faber 15)
HAPPY BIRTHDAY, WANDA JUNE - Kurt Vonnegut, Jr.	Harper (50)	1:15	I, 4	When Penelope asked me to... (Dell 56)
HAPPY BIRTHDAY, WANDA JUNE - Kurt Vonnegut, Jr.	Von Konigswald (50, Nazi)	3:00	I, 7	I am Major Siegfried von... (Dell 76)

HARVEY Mary Chase	Elwood (47)	1:30	I, 1	Excuse me a moment. I have to... (DPS 4)
HEY YOU, LIGHT MAN! Oliver Hailey	Knight (middle-age)	1:45	II	But the boy, once when he was...* (DPS 58)
HONOUR AND OFFER Henry Livings	Henry (50s, English)	1:45	I	The bees burble gently... (Methuen 34)
THE HOUSE OF BLUE LEAVES - John Guare	Bananas (45)	1:45	I	My troubles all began... (SF 31)
JUMPERS Tom Stoppard	George (40s, English)	3:00	I	Consider my left sock. (Grove 28)
JUMPERS Tom Stoppard	George (40s, English)	8:00	I	Professor McFee's introductory... (Grove 52)
JUMPERS Tom Stoppard	George (40s, English)	3:00	II	How does one know... (Grove 71)
LAST OF THE RED HOT LOVERS - Neil Simon	Barney (47)	3:30	I	Just sit there! (SF 28)
THE LESSON - Eugene Ionesco - in "Four Plays"	Professor (50s)	2:00	1-act	As for the neo-Spanish... (Grove 64)
LOVERS (LOSERS) Brian Friel	Andy (50, Irish)	4:00	sc. 2	The big mistake I made... (Dram 103)
LOVERS AND OTHER STRANGERS - Taylor & Bologna	Frank (45-55)	1:15	4	I love your mother, but... (SF 37)
LOVERS AND OTHER STRANGERS - Taylor & Bologna	Frank (45-55)	1:15	4	More. More. You think I don't... (SF 39)
THE MATCHMAKER Thornton Wilder	Malachi (50)	2:00	III	A purse. That fellow over there... (SF 76)
THE MIKADO (MUSICAL) W.S. Gilbert	Pooh-bah (middle-age)	1:45	I	I am, in point of fact...* (Schirmer 9)
MIXED DOUBLES George Melly	The Vicar (50s)	2:00	I	It seems but yesterday... (Methuen 11)
MORNING - Israel Horovitz - in "Morning, Noon & Night"	Tillich (40s)	1:00	sc. 4	I never would have... (SF 17)
NEXT Terrence McNally	Marion (40)	5:00	1-act	Oh don't worry, I'm going. (DPS 48)
PLAZA SUITE Neil Simon	Jesse (40)	2:00	II	Muriel, I don't know what...* (SF 60)
PRESENT LAUGHTER Noel Coward	Garry (50s, English)	1:15	III	I'm sick to death of being... (SF 96)
THE PUBLIC EYE Peter Shaffer	Charles (40, English)	2:00	1-act	Yes...It was a curious courtship.* (SF 19)
PYGMALION Bernard Shaw	Doolittle (50s, Cockney)	4:00	V	Oh! Drunk am?!* (Penguin 92)
ROMANOFF AND JULIET Peter Ustinov	General (40s)	2:00	I	Why? The only one who's always... (DPS 15)
ROMANOFF AND JULIET Peter Ustinov	Romanoff (50s, Russian)	1:45	II	We have a perfect right... (DPS 46)
ROMANOFF AND JULIET Peter Ustinov	General (40s)	1:45	III	Now, maybe a short historical... (DPS 64)
SCENES FROM AMERICAN LIFE - A.R. Gurney, Jr.	Man (50s)	1:15	II	Dear Brad. Thanks for your note. (SF 52)
A SCENT OF FLOWERS James Saunders	Edgar (middle-age)	2:15	I	At the moment of my conception... (DPS 14)
SCUBA DUBA Bruce Jay Friedman	Tourist (middle-age)	2:00	I	Now that's the kind of talk... (DPS 10)
THE SHOCK OF RECOGNITION - Robert Anderson - in "You Know I Can't Hear You When the Water's Running"	Pawling (40s)	1:15	1-act	Oh...How do you do...* (DPS 16)

A SLIGHT ACHE Harold Pinter	Edward (middle-age, English)	8:00	1-act	Here I am. Where are you? (Grove 22)
SUMMER IN THE COUNTRY Anton Chekhov	Tolkachov (40, Russian)	6:00	1-act	Bad? You can't see... (SF 58)
THE TEAHOUSE OF THE AUGUST MOON John Patrick	Sakini (30-60, Okinawan)	2:30	I, 1	Juicy-fruit. Most generous gift... (DPS 5)
TEVYA AND HIS DAUGHTERS - Arnold Perl	Tevya (50, Jewish)	1:45	I, 2	So, horse, we ride... (DPS 13)
TEVYA AND HIS DAUGHTERS - Arnold Perl	Tevya (50, Jewish)	1:30	II	Well, horse, we had a good day. (DPS 28)
A THOUSAND CLOWNS Herb Gardner	Arnold (early 40s)	1:30	III	Wow, I scared myself. (SF 76)
TOUR - Terrence McNally - in "Apple Pie"	Mr. Wilson (40s)	1:30	sc. 4	I guess you people get some...* (DPS 8)
THE UGLY DUCKLING A.A. Milne	King (middle-age)	2:30	1-act	It is our little plan...* (SFL 15)
WELCOME TO THE MONKEY HOUSE Christopher Sergel	George (40s)	1:30	I	Gave me a whole series that time. (Dram 5)
WHAT THE BUTLER SAW Joe Orton	Rance (50s)	1:00	II	Lunatics are melodramatic. (SF 54)

60 AND OVER

THE DOCK BRIEF John Mortimer	Morgenhall (60s, English)	2:00	sc. 2	He's not here at the moment... (SFL 24)
THE DOCK BRIEF John Mortimer	Morgenhall (60s, English)	1:15	sc. 2	There's a different atmosphere...* (SFL 30)
FLINT David Mercer	The Bishop (70, English)	3:00	I, 6	In these turbulent years... (Methuen 40)
FORTY YEARS ON Alan Bennett	Headmaster (60s, English)	6:30	I	Members of Albion House... (Faber 12)
LITTLE MURDERS Jules Feiffer	Judge (60s)	4:45	I, 2	Sit down please. (SF 31)
THE MATCHMAKER Thornton Wilder	Horace (60)	2:15	I	Ninety-nine percent of the people... (SF 18)
NOURISH THE BEAST Steve Tesich	Old Man	1:45	II, 2	Once and for all... (SF 52)
SPOFFORD Herman Shumlin	Spofford (70)	2:15	I	What you see before you is...* (SF 7)
THE SUNSHINE BOYS Neil Simon	Willie (70s)	1:30	I, 1	Eleven years ago on...* (SF 19)
THE TIME OF YOUR LIFE William Saroyan	Kit Carson (70)	2:45	II	Down in Gallup, twenty years ago.* (SF 97)

MODERN MALE SERIO-COMIC

UNDER 20

AH, WILDERNESS! Eugene O'Neill	Richard (16)	2:15	III, 2	Gosh, that music from the hotel... (SF 108)
ENTERTAINING MR. SLOANE - Joe Orton	Sloane (17, English)	1:30	II	I trust you, Pop. (Grove 58)

TAKE A GIANT STEP Louis Peterson	Spence (17, Black)	1:45	I, 1	Well - from the very beginning...* (SF 13)

20 - 30

CAMELOT (MUSICAL) Alan Jay Lerner	Arthur (mid- 20s, English)	1:30	I, 1	When I was a lad of eighteen... (Dell 175)
GOIN' A BUFFALO Ed Bullins	Art (23, Black)	3:30	I, 3	You see...it was about three...* (B-M 38)
HAIL SCRAWDYKE! David Halliwell	Nipple (26, North Country English)	3:00	sc. 4	Women respond t' me... (Grove 68)
HALLOWEEN - Leonard Melfi - in "Encounters"	Luke (almost 30)	4:30	1-act	Hey, what the hell's going on... (RH 81)
THE JOURNEY OF THE FIFTH HORSE - Ronald Ribman	Chulkaturin (20s)	1:15	II	How well the conversation proceeds... (SF 56)
LUNCHTIME - Leonard Melfi - in "Encounters"	Rex (27)	1:30	1-act	My wife's name is Geraldine... (RH 61)
LUNCHTIME - Leonard Melfi - in "Encounters"	Rex (27)	1:30	1-act	Good...I wish Gerry drank... (RH 62)
MUZEEKA John Guare	Argue (20s)	5:30	1-act	If I could've been born... (DPS 6)
PARADISE GARDENS EAST Frank Gagliano	Brother (late 20s)	1:45	1-act	THERE ARE HORRORS OUT THERE. (DPS 11)
PARADISE GARDENS EAST Frank Gagliano	O'Neill	3:15	1-act	It is now the incinerator hour...* (DPS 16)
THE PEOPLE VS. RANCHMAN - Megan Terry	Ranchman (20s)	1:30	Epilogue	I want to thank you... (SF 42)
PHILADELPHIA, HERE I COME! - Brian Friel	Private (20s, Irish)	1:30	III, 1	What the hell had you... (SF 71)
THE PRIVATE EAR Peter Shaffer	Tchaik (20s, English)	1:00	1-act	Benjamin Britten! Like me.* (SF 23)
RING ROUND THE MOON Jean Anouilh	Hugo (20s)	2:30	III, 1	There's no doubt you're still... (DPS 57)
SLOW DANCE ON THE KILLING GROUND William Hanley	Randall (20s, Black)	6:00	I	True, all true. Truly. (DPS 28)
SWEET EROS Terrence McNally	Young Man	2:15	sc. 6	The happiest day of my life? (DPS 16)
THE TIME OF YOUR LIFE William Saroyan	Willie (20)	1:30	V	Oh, boy! There you are, Nick. (SF 157)
TIME REMEMBERED Jean Anouilh	Albert (25)	5:00	II, 1	Life is a wonderful thing to talk...* (SF 57)

30 - 40

CUBA SI! Terrence McNally	Reporter (30)	2:30	1-act	You're staying? But there's not... (DPS 16)
INDIANS Arthur Kopit	Sitting Bull (30s, Indian)	2:15	sc. 11	I shall tell you, then... (H&W 70)
INDIANS Arthur Kopit	Buffalo Bill (30s)	4:30	sc. 13	NOT YET!...I would... (H&W 89)
JACK, OR THE SUBMISSION - Eugene Ionesco	Jack (30s)	2:30	1-act	When I was born, I was almost... (Grove 103)
JOE EGG Peter Nichols	Bri (33, English)	3:00	I	What's his speciality? (Grove 24)
LONG DAY'S JOURNEY INTO NIGHT - Eugene O'Neill	Jamie (33)	2:00	IV	No joke. Very serious.* (Yale 159)

MUZEEKA John Guare	#2 (30s)	1:00	1-act	You write that Muzeeka, huh? (DPS 25)
THE NIGHT OF THE IGUANA - Tennessee Williams	Shannon (35)	2:15	II	Miss Jelkes, you're still not... (DPS 74)
OLD TIMES Harold Pinter	Deeley (30s, English)	1:45	I	What happened to me was this. (Grove 29)
OLD TIMES Harold Pinter	Deeley (30s, English)	2:00	II	Of course we've met before.* (Grove 50)
THE RAINMAKER N. Richard Nash	Starbuck (30s)	1:30	I	What do you care how... (SF 41)
ROSENCRANTZ AND GUILDENSTERN ARE DEAD Tom Stoppard	Guildenstern (30s, English)	2:15	I	The scientific approach to... (SF 12)
THE SHOCK OF RECOGNITION - Robert Anderson - in "You Know I Can't Hear You When the Water's Running"	Jack (30s)	1:15	1-act	This one moment is... (DPS 15)
A THOUSAND CLOWNS Herb Gardner	Murray (mid-30s)	1:15	II	Tell you the truth... (SF 51)
A THOUSAND CLOWNS Herb Gardner	Murray (mid-30s)	1:15	III	Oh, Arnie, you don't understand... (SF 75)
THE ZOO STORY Edward Albee	Jerry (late 30s)	10:00	1-act	ALL RIGHT. THE STORY OF JERRY... (DPS 15)

40 - 60

AH, WILDERNESS! Eugene O'Neill	Nat (59)	1:45	III, 3	But listen here, Richard, hmm... (SF 126)
ANTIGONE Jean Anouilh	Creon (50s)	2:45	-	The pride of Oedipus! (SF 45)
BORSTAL BOY Frank McMahon	Behan (40, Irish)	1:15	I	That poor fellow was a Dubliner... (SF 10)
CHILDREN OF THE WIND Jerry Devine	Brophy (40s)	1:00	I, 1	Good evening. (DPS 5)
DEAR LIAR Jerome Kilty	Shaw (40s, English)	3:00	I	What a day! I must write... (SF 19)
EQUUS Peter Shaffer	Dysart (40s, English)	1:30	sc. 18	Do you know what... (Deutsch 60)
FATHER UXBRIDGE WANTS TO MARRY - Frank Gagliano	Ongar (middle-age)	4:00	1-act	The abyss. You fear the abyss. (DPS 36)
THE FOOTSTEPS OF DOVES Robert Anderson - in "You Know I Can't Hear You When the Water's Running"	George (50s)	1:30	1-act	Now people are detached.* (DPS 26)
THE GOOD DOCTOR Neil Simon	Writer (40s)	5:00	I, 1	It's quite all right... (RH 3)
HUGHIE - Eugene O'Neill - in "The Later Plays"	Erie (early 40s)	3:00	1-act	Yeah. Hughie was one... (RH 275)
IN THE WINE TIME Ed Bullins	Cliff (40s, Black)	2:00	II	I just need to take one look...* (B-M 154)
JOHNNAS Bill Gunn	Barney (middle- age, Black)	3:00	1-act	Well, Philly's not bad... (TDR 40, p. 129)
LOVERS (LOSERS) Brian Friel	Andy (50, Irish)	2:30	sc. 1	I'll tell you something... (Dram 78)
MAN AND SUPERMAN Bernard Shaw	The Devil	4:00	III	And is Man any the less... (Penguin 142)
THE MUNDY SCHEME Brian Friel	Ryan (40s, Irish)	2:30	III, 1	I want to talk to you tonight... (SF 56)

THE ONLY GAME IN TOWN - Frank D. Gilroy	Lockwood (55)	1:45	I, 7	Open this door! Open it! (SF 45)
OUR TOWN Thornton Wilder	Stage Manager (middle-age, New England)	2:30	I	This play is called "Our Town." (SF 1)
THE ROPE DANCERS Morton Wishengrad	James (middle-age)	1:30	I	Just now we spoke of hunger... (SF 21)
SATURDAY, SUNDAY, MONDAY - Eduardo de Filippo; adapt: Waterhouse & Hall	Peppino (50s)	2:00	III	Jealousy, Rosi. (Heinemann 80)
STEAMBATH Bruce Jay Friedman	Tandy (early 40s)	2:30	II	I got friends, terrific friends. (SF 60)
TEA PARTY Harold Pinter	Sisson (late 40s, English)	2:00	sc. 7	I think I should explain to you...* (DPS 12)
TEVYA AND HIS DAUGHTERS - Arnold Perl	Tevya (50, Jewish)	3:00	II	Only a fool is not afraid...* (DPS 46)
U.S.A. - Paul Shyre & John Dos Passos	Player C (middle-age)	3:00	II	The nineteen-year-old son... (SF 54)

60 AND OVER

THE BEAUTIFUL PEOPLE William Saroyan	Jonah (60s)	2:30	II, 2	I wouldn't be able to speak...* (SF 96)
CAT ON A HOT TIN ROOF Tennessee Williams	Big Daddy (60s, Southern)	3:00	II	We got that clock the summer...* (DPS 41)
ENEMIES Arkady Leokum	Miller (60s)	2:00	1-act	No...Not because I'm... (SF 22)
THE FLOWERING PEACH Clifford Odets	Noah (70s)	2:30	sc. 1	Lonely times again... (DPS 11)
FRIENDS Arkady Leokum	The Teacher (65)	2:30	1-act	All right, all right, all right! (SF 30)
THE HOMECOMING Harold Pinter	Max (70s)	2:30	II	Well, it's a long time since.... (Grove 45)
IN WHITE AMERICA Martin Duberman	Tillman (old, Southern)	3:15	II	Mr. President, a word about lynching... (SF 50)
JUNK YARD Lewis John Carlino	Simon (65)	1:30	1-act	You know when I first decided... (DPS 15)
THE RIMERS OF ELDRITCH Lanford Wilson	Skelly (60s)	3:00	II	Hound? Hey, hound. What are you... (DPS 37)
STEAMBATH Bruce Jay Friedman	The Oldtimer	1:00	II	Well, that's OK. I done everything. (SF 45)

ONE CHARACTER PLAYS

FEMALE SERIOUS

BEFORE BREAKFAST Eugene O'Neill - in "Six Short Plays"	Mrs. Rowland (20s)	10:00	one-act	(RH 4)
THE STRONGER - August Strindberg - in "Six Plays"	Mrs. X (30s)	10:00	one-act	(Doubleday 117)

FEMALE COMIC

ANIMAL - Oliver Hailey - in "Picture, Animal, Crisscross"; also in "Collision Course," p. 75	The Woman (middle-age)	4:30	one-act	(DPS 25)

FEMALE SERIO-COMIC

LAUGHS, ETC. - James Leo Herlihy - in "Stop! You're Killing Me"	Gloria (40)	12:00	one-act	(DPS 7)
ONE WOMAN SHOW Cornelia Otis Skinner	various	various	-	(Dram)

MALE SERIOUS

DAYS AHEAD - Lanford Wilson - in "Rimers of Eldritch and Other Plays"	Man (45)	10:00	one-act	(H&W 65)
PASSPORT - James Elward - in "Friday Night"	Charlie (41)	15:00	one-act	(DPS 27)
TERRIBLE JIM FITCH James Leo Herlihy - in "Stop! You're Killing Me"	Jim Fitch (30s)	25:00	one-act	(DPS 19)

MALE COMIC

THE HARMFULNESS OF TOBACCO - Anton Chekhov - in "The Brute and Other Farces"	Lecturer (50-60)	7:00	one-act	(SF 3)

MALE SERIO-COMIC

BRIEF LIVES John Aubrey	Aubrey (old)	about 2 hours	full-length	(Faber)
THE OLD JEW - Murray Schisgal - in "Five Plays"	The Old Jew (30)	15:00	one-act	(DPS 101)

OTHER BOOKS OF INTEREST
FROM DRAMA BOOK PUBLISHERS

Edited by Jane Grumbach and Robert Emerson
ACTORS GUIDE TO MONOLOGUES, VOLUME 2: REVISED
ACTORS GUIDE TO SCENES
MONOLOGUES: MEN
MONOLOGUES: MEN, VOLUME 2
MONOLOGUES: WOMEN
MONOLOGUES: WOMEN, VOLUME 2

The Classical Monologues Series, edited by Stefan Rudnicki
CLASSICAL MONOLOGUES 1: SHAKESPEARE
CLASSICAL MONOLOGUES 2: SHAKESPEARE & FRIENDS
CLASSICAL MONOLOGUES 3: THE AGE OF STYLE
CLASSICAL MONOLOGUES 4: SHAKESPEARE & FRIENDS ENCORE
CLASSICAL MONOLOGUES 5: WARHORSES

Books on acting, voice, and speech
FREEING THE NATURAL VOICE by Kristin Linklater
THE USE AND TRAINING OF THE HUMAN VOICE by Arthur Lessac
BODY WISDOM: THE USE AND TRAINING OF THE HUMAN BODY by Arthur Lessac
GOOD SPEECH FOR THE AMERICAN ACTOR by Edith Skinner and Timothy Monich
THE PROFESSIONAL ACTOR: FROM AUDITION TO PERFORMANCE by Tom Markus

Write for our free catalogue: DRAMA BOOK PUBLISHERS, 821 Broadway,
New York, New York 10003.

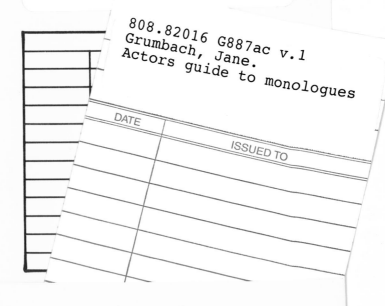